BRITAIN IN OLD PHOTOGRAPHS

WARWICKSHIRE RAILWAYS

MIKE HITCHES

SUTTON PUBLISHING LIMITED

Sutton Publishing Limited
Phoenix Mill · Thrupp · Stroud
Gloucestershire · GL5 2BU

First published 1997

British Library Cataloguing in Publication Data
A catalogue record for this book is available from the
British Library.

ISBN 0-7509-1366-5

Typeset in 10/12 Perpetua.
Typesetting and origination by
Sutton Publishing Limited.
Printed in Great Britain by
Ebenezer Baylis, Worcester.

TO JO AND ROY

CONTENTS

An ex-GWR Collett 'Hall' class 4–6–0 enters Tyseley station with an express from Oxford to Birmingham (Snow Hill) in the late 1950s. The station entrance and booking hall are situated in the building on the overbridge above the locomotive.

INTRODUCTION

The first railway to serve Warwickshire was the London and Birmingham Railway, which opened in 1838. This was built to provide a link between the fast-growing industrial town of Birmingham (later to become Britain's second city) and the capital and to tap potentially lucrative freight and passenger traffic. The L&B became part of the London and North Western Railway in 1846. Its General Manager, Captain Mark Huish, became embroiled in some very dirty tricks as he tried everything to prevent the Great Western Railway from bringing its own broad gauge line from London (Paddington) to Birmingham (Snow Hill). Ironically, Huish, as Secretary of the Grand Junction Railway, had proposed in the early 1840s that a joint project for a line from Paddington to Birmingham, via Rugby, be set up to apply pressure on the L&B who were keen on the proposed Trent Valley Railway. This had the potential to take traffic away from the GJR at Birmingham, as the new line would avoid the town altogether. In the event the GWR succeeded in completing its own route, despite the efforts of Huish, and it opened to traffic in 1852. Thus, Warwickshire had two railway routes for Birmingham and London which provided competition between the LNWR, LMS and GWR for many years, although the L&B was always the more important line.

These two main lines served some prominent towns within the county. The L&B ran through Coventry and Rugby, while the GWR route passed Warwick and Leamington Spa. The Paddington company also had a branch from Hatton, bound for Bristol, which ran through the famous Shakespearean town of Stratford-upon-Avon. This was also served by the Midland Railway line from Woodford to Broom Junction (as the Stratford-upon-Avon and Midland Junction Railway). Leamington Spa was considered important to the railway companies, as it was already a well-established resort town. As the GWR line progressed towards Birmingham, the LNWR built its own branch to the town from Coventry in 1842, extending the line to Rugby in 1851. Rugby, at this time, was already a junction, the Trent Valley Railway having opened in 1847. This line ran from Rugby to Stafford and served the important manufacturing town of Nuneaton, as well as coal-mining districts in Warwickshire. Nuneaton itself was also served by the Midland Railway, whose line from Birmingham to Leicester, via

Nuneaton, opened in 1864. There was also an LNWR line from Nuneaton to Coventry, still very much in existence.

From 1899, Rugby faced competition from another company, the Great Central Railway, whose main line between London (Marylebone), Sheffield and Manchester passed through the county here. The GCR also had some influence on the GWR in Warwickshire when proposals were brought forward to construct the Birmingham and North Warwickshire Railway. This was to run from Birmingham (Moor Street) to Stratford-upon-Avon, where it would join the GWR branch to Alcester and the main line to Bristol, as well as the East and West Junction Railway line which ran from the GCR at Woodford to Evesham. The GCR were keen to operate this line for access to Birmingham and to open up another access to London. In the event, the Marylebone company agreed terms with the GWR for the construction of a joint line from Banbury to London, thereby benefiting both companies. Therefore, there was no need to support the B&NW. This line was eventually built by the GWR, opening at the end of 1907, who used the line as a shorter route from Birmingham to Bristol and the West Country, making for better competition with the Midland Railway route, via Bromsgrove. With the completion of the B&NW, the railway network in Warwickshire was complete, surviving virtually intact until Dr Beeching began wielding his infamous axe.

As the railway network developed, Birmingham businessmen moved out of the smoky town into rural Warwickshire and the new suburbs, creating a need for local commuter trains. These same businessmen would travel to London or between, perhaps, Coventry and Rugby, all these journeys requiring trains. There was a thriving tourist market for the railways to tap into, day excursions to such places as Leamington, Stratford-upon-Avon and Henley-in-Arden, as well as long-distance holiday destinations like the West Country and the Lancashire coast. The industrial nature of towns like Birmingham, Coventry, Rugby and Nuneaton, as well as the Warwickshire coalfields, generated a great deal of freight traffic for the railways, with plenty of work for all the competing companies.

With so much traffic in the county, all manner of steam locomotives could be seen at the head of trains on the local railway network, from humble 0–6–0 tank engines on local passenger and goods work to top link express types. On the L&B line, LNWR 4–4–0s operated express services until replaced by LMS Stanier 'Jubilee' class 4–6–0s on Birmingham–Euston services. Rugby and the TVR saw the very best of LNWR and LMS express engines, including early 2–2–2 'Bloomer' locos of the mid-nineteenth century, LNWR 4–6–0s of 'Experiment', 'Prince of Wales' and 'Claughton' classes, along with others. In LMS days, 'Princess-Royal' and 'Duchess' Pacifics operated Euston–Glasgow expresses. Freight was handled by heavy LNWR 0–8–0s 'Black Five' 4–6–0s and 8F 2–8–0s. The GCR at Rugby saw Robinson 4–6–0s and LNER types on expresses, as well as GCR and LNER tank and freight locos. The GWR also had its famous engines over its lines in Warwickshire. The Paddington–Birkenhead expresses ran through the county with double-framed 4–4–0s through to 'Castle' and 'King' class 4–6–0s at the head of these trains. The B&NW also saw 'Star' and 'Castle' class 4–6–0s on West Country trains, although these services were initially operated by 'County' class 4–4–0s. Freight was often in the hands of '28xx' class 2–8–0s or 'Hall' class 4–6–0s. Local trains were usually headed by 0–6–0 pannier tanks or 2–6–2 prairie tanks. To supply locos for many of these services, the county was provided with locosheds at places like Coventry, Rugby, Nuneaton, Leamington Spa, Tyseley and Warwick.

Following nationalization, the railway system in Warwickshire underwent many changes, not least with the introduction of modern traction in the 1950s. Diesel Multiple Unit trains began to operate local services from the mid-1950s and diesel-electric locos operated express trains at roughly the same time on ex-LNWR routes. On the ex-GWR network, diesel-hydraulic traction was used on Paddington–Birkenhead expresses. By the mid-1960s, traffic on the old L&B and TVR became electric hauled, thanks to an investment of millions in the electrification of the West Coast main line.

Rationalization of the railway network within the county was undertaken following the Beeching Reshaping Report. The B&NW was scheduled for closure when West Country traffic was transferred to the ex-Midland Railway main line from Birmingham (New Street) in 1967. The B&NW, however, survives as a commuter line only. The GWR main line lost much of its express traffic between Birmingham (Snow Hill) and Paddington after the LNWR main line from New Street to Euston was electrified in 1967. Snow Hill station was closed, but it survived for commuter trains operating out of Birmingham (Moor Street). However, Snow Hill station was reopened in the late 1980s and a new semi-express service now runs over the route from Snow Hill to the ex-GCR station at Marylebone, offering a 2½ hour service between Birmingham and London. The GCR main line was closed completely in the mid-1960s.

Although the old GWR system in Warwickshire took the brunt of the cuts, the ex-LNWR lines did not escape unscathed; the Leamington–Weedon line closed in 1959 and the Leamington–Coventry line closed to passengers in 1965. The Midland Railway system has largely survived, apart from the line through Stratford-upon-Avon, which closed to passengers in 1951. It survived for freight traffic, however, until 1964.

The companies who operated trains through Warwickshire left a legacy of different architectural styles which have provided a great variety of stations to serve the communities through which their railways ran. Along with the many locomotive types that operated trains within the county, these differences created much of interest. In preparing this volume, I have gained a great deal of pleasure from selecting the photographs for inclusion because of the sheer diversity of the locations. I sincerely hope that you, the reader, derive just as much pleasure from the material as I have had in putting it all together.

THE LONDON & BIRMINGHAM RAILWAY

The first railway line in the county of Warwickshire, the London and Birmingham Railway, was opened on Sunday 24 June 1838. It met the Grand Junction Railway, opened a year earlier, at Birmingham and provided a railway link between the important seaport at Liverpool, the cotton city of Manchester and the capital, via the rapidly growing industrial town of Birmingham.

Plans for a railway between London and Birmingham were proposed as early as 1808 by one William Jones, who suggested a network of railways to cover the whole nation. In 1822, Jones actually surveyed a route between the two destinations, his line to run via Oxford. Although his project was a little premature, it was basically sound and was practically identical to the one planned by Sir John Rennie when he presented his proposal to Parliament on 1 April 1826. The one major drawback of Rennie's plan was that it missed out the important cloth-weaving city of Coventry, running as proposed, via Southam, some two miles south. What finally wrecked Rennie's plan, however, was the difficulty in financing such a project when money was not as freely available as it had been previously. Nothing was done again until 1829.

At that time, Francis Giles, an engineer for twenty years, surveyed a route which ran via Coventry instead of Oxford. This was the one chosen when influential men at Coventry consulted Robert Stephenson, who favoured a line with their interests in mind. Soon afterwards, Robert, and his father George, were appointed as engineers to the newly formed London and Birmingham Railway Company. A Bill was presented to Parliament in 1832, but was fiercely opposed by landowners who sought a better price than the one offered by the company. After these landowners had been 'bought off', a second Bill was promoted the following year and given Royal Assent on 6 May 1833. On the same day, the GJR was also given parliamentary approval for its line.

The section of the L&B between Birmingham and Rugby was opened on 9 April 1838, with intermediate stations at Hampton (becoming Hampton-in-Arden in 1886), Brandon and Coventry, all trains leaving from Birmingham Curzon Street station. The line also opened between Euston and Denbigh Hall (1¼ miles north of Bletchley) on the same day, the two sections being linked by stagecoach until Kilsby Tunnel was completed. After spending some £300,000 on its construction, the tunnel was opened on 21 June 1838, completing the whole route between London and Birmingham.

When train services began, the locomotives used were supplied by Edmund Bury and were characterized by their 'haycock' fireboxes. These engines were 2–2–0s and a total of fifty-eight had been supplied by 1841. Train speeds then were certainly slow, the L&B deciding that 20 m.p.h. was quite fast enough, and a journey from Euston to Birmingham would take 5 hours 38 minutes, compared to 12 hours by the fastest stagecoaches. It was, however, enough to attract large numbers of passengers and great quantities of freight, making the line very successful.

The L&B has certainly stood the test of time; today it is still the main route for trains operating between London (Euston) and Birmingham (New Street). The only real changes to occur in the intervening years were that Curzon Street ceased to be used when Birmingham New Street station opened on 1 June 1854; a brand new station, Birmingham International, was opened in February 1976 to serve the National Exhibition Centre and Birmingham International Airport; and Coventry station was completely rebuilt when the route was electrified in the mid-1960s.

Curzon Street station, the northern terminus of the London and Birmingham Railway, as it appeared shortly after opening when services between Rugby and Birmingham commenced on 9 April 1838. The line was not fully opened as far as London (Euston) until June of the same year. The station was designed by Philip Hardwick who was responsible for the famous Doric Arch at Euston, which was so cruelly destroyed when the new 'antiseptic' Euston was built in the 1960s. Curzon Street station was fronted by a monumental portico which was meant to symbolize the railway company's ambition to be regarded as a grand entrance to the world beyond. The station was shared with the Grand Junction Railway, whose own route from Birmingham (Vauxhall) to Earlestown – where it met the Liverpool and Manchester Railway, opened in 1829 – had been opened a year earlier. To gain access to Curzon Street, the GJR built a spur from Vauxhall and its old station became a goods yard. Joint use of Curzon Street facilitated an interchange of traffic between the two companies, thereby creating a direct link between two important north-west cities and London, with Birmingham as the hub, although the rapidly expanding industrial towns' demands were soon to be substantial in themselves. By the time the L&B and GJR, along with the Trent Valley and Manchester and Birmingham Railways, became the London and North Western Railway on 16 July 1846, Curzon Street was becoming inadequate for current traffic demands. It was also in an inconvenient location, a little way out of the town centre. Thus, a new station was to be built closer to the centre and Curzon Street was to be abandoned. The new station, Birmingham New Street, was opened on 1 June 1854 and Curzon Street closed to all LNWR traffic on 1 July. It was, however, retained for use by the Midland Railway until 1893 when it closed altogether. The great portico was kept in the centre of a goods yard and used as offices for many years. By the mid-1960s, BR could find no further use for the building and planned its demolition. Birmingham City Council stepped in, bought the building for £5 and restoration was undertaken. Thus the fine entrance to Curzon Street station still stands and it can be seen, on the left, from London-bound trains after leaving the tunnel from New Street station.

The interior of Curzon Street's replacement, New Street station, seen here in LNWR days. The station appears busy with several trains in view, one of which is hauled by an LNWR tank loco. Almost as soon as the LNWR had been incorporated, the company presented the L&B with a (Birmingham Extension) Bill for a line of just under a mile long from the terminus at Curzon Street to a proposed new station at what was to be New Street, but at that time was to be called Navigation Street. The line was to cost £25,000 and was engineered by Robert Stephenson who constructed a tunnel of 273 yards, which ran under the town to bring the line into the new station. The Act authorizing a new station was given Royal Assent on 3 August and stipulated that, as the station would obliterate King Street, one of the main roads in the town, a footpath, which must be open to the public at all times, must run through the station. Thus, New Street was an 'open' station until it was rebuilt in the 1960s.

An ex-LNWR 'George the Fifth' class 4–4–0 no. 5354 (LNWR No. 2081) *New Zealand* waits at Birmingham New Street in LMS days. By the time the LMS had inherited New Street it had lost much of its original splendour and one passenger commented, in 1923: 'It is on a cold, wet night that the station reaches its most repulsive, it is ill-lit by a faulty gas system, devoid of adequate seating, the roof leaks in countless places, and the lavatories proclaim their presence.' Modern-day passengers also complain about the 1960s-built edifice, complaining of its draughtiness and dinginess.

Back in the glory days of New Street station and LNWR 2–2–2 loco no. 311 *Richard Francis Roberts*, a Webb Compound, waits at the station in 1903.

On 16 July 1920, two-and-a-half years before the 'grouping' which brought the LMS into existence, two LNWR locos, 'Jumbo' 2–4–0 no. 514 *Puck* on the left and 'Precursor' 4–4–0 no. 218 *Daphne* on the right, wait with their respective trains at New Street. The station was extended to accommodate the Midland Railway in 1885, both sections having huge arched roofs made of glass and iron. The LNWR side of the station suffered bomb damage during the Second World War which added further to its general shabbiness. By 1964, such was the state of the place that Sir Arthur Smout, former President of Birmingham Chamber of Commerce, was moved to comment in 1964: 'I know of no station in this country, Europe, or the USA which for filth, muck, and general dishevelment compares with New Street.' Shortly afterwards, the new station was built as part of the West Coast main line electrification and it opened in 1966. The new station, however, is just as unpopular and seems almost 'dungeon-like'.

Stechford station as it appears since electrification was completed in 1966. Stechford was, at one time, an important junction when, in 1882, the Stechford–Aston line was opened. This line relieved pressure on the Stour Valley line, which ran from New Street to Wolverhampton High Level station, by allowing the diversion of some Wolverhampton expresses away from New Street. These trains were divided at Stechford, the front portions continuing, via Aston and the Grand Junction Railway, to Wolverhampton while the rear portions called at New Street and all stations to Wolverhampton.

Post-electrification Lea Hall station. Note the modern, 1960s-style station buildings and platform awnings.

Marston Green station, near Birmingham airport. The station is seen here at the commencement of electrification work. In this view, the station buildings are of wooden construction and appear to be the original LNWR design.

Electric trains wait at Birmingham International station. The station was built to serve the new National Exhibition Centre, opened by Her Majesty the Queen on 2 February 1976, and Birmingham International Airport. Birmingham International railway station was the first new station to be built this century and has fully justified its existence ever since. The station is very busy during the summer holiday season and when the International Motor Show is on. Visitors to the Motor Show prefer to use the trains rather than find car-parking space at the centre. Very often, the railway companies offer combined rail travel and Motor Show tickets. Incidentally, the station connects with Birmingham Airport's 'Maglev' monorail system for access to airport terminals.

Hampton-in-Arden station as it appeared in the days of steam. The station was opened with the L&B and was originally named 'Hampton', the 'in-Arden' being added in 1886. The station was once a junction with the Birmingham and Derby Junction Railway, incorporated on 19 May 1836. Originally, the B&DJR was to form a junction with the L&B at Stechford, but eventually met the L&B at Hampton, via a 6 mile branch from Whitacre. The B&DJR eventually had its own line between Whitacre and Birmingham (Lawley Street) from 1842 and, as part of the Midland Railway, gained access to New Street in 1854. The line from Whitacre to Hampton survived for passenger traffic until 1 January 1917. It closed to goods traffic in April 1930.

Hampton-in-Arden station following electrification. The imposing main buildings have gone, replaced by simple waiting shelters.

Tile Hill station, Coventry, as it appeared in steam days, complete with BR London–Midland Region station nameboard. Along with the simple wooden station buildings, the goods yard is also in view. This was closed on 4 February 1963, at a time when the L&B line was being prepared for electrification.

Canley Halt, Coventry, following electrification. The wooden signal cabin, a throwback to steam days, is visible in the distance.

Coventry station, showing the main L&B line on the left and the line to Kenilworth and Leamington (Avenue) curving away to the right. Coventry locoshed can be seen beyond the signal-box. There has been a station at Coventry since the opening of the L&B and the city's railway system was under complete control of the LNWR. This was because only two routes other than the L&B radiated from the city; a useful link to Nuneaton and the line to Leamington, both under the control of Euston. When the L&B first opened, Coventry was provided with a totally inadequate station which was replaced in 1840. This station was enlarged several times, including an extension authorized for the LMS in 1935. The station suffered bomb damage during the Blitz on the city in 1941 and it had become cramped and dirty by the early 1960s. Coventry station was demolished, and replaced by a new glass and concrete structure in 1962 as part of WCML electrification.

A similar view to the one above, after electrification was complete. The old locoshed and wooden signal-box have disappeared from the landscape and have been replaced by a brick, concrete and glass power signal-box. Overhead power lines now dominate the scene.

Ex-LNWR 7F 0–8–0, BR no. 49125 runs through Coventry station on 25 May 1953 with an empty stock train. Coventry played a significant role during the building of the L&B when Robert Stephenson used the city as his headquarters during construction of the Birmingham–Rugby section.

On a freight working through Coventry is ex-LMS 'Fairburn' 2–6–4 tank loco no. 42674, seen here on 25 May 1953.

Coventry locoshed as it appeared in the mid-1950s. The main shed building is on the right and the coaling stage is on the left. Behind is an advertisement for the *Coventry Evening Telegraph*. A shed was first proposed for Coventry in 1865 and a two-road brick-built structure was completed in 1866 in the fork between the Rugby and Warwick lines. The shed was doubled in size in 1897 and was provided with a 42-ft turntable. Its allocation reached a peak of about twenty locos in the 1930s and it was always a sub-shed of Rugby. The shed provided engines for local workings, mainly mineral traffic. During the 1941 Blitz the shed remained largely undamaged, but had to be closed on more than one occasion because of unexploded bombs. The 42-ft turntable was replaced by the LMS, a 57-ft model being introduced. By the 1950s the shed was somewhat dilapidated, its roof being in very poor condition. A new one made of corrugated sheeting was provided by BR. The shed survived until 17 November 1958, but it remained as a store for condemned locos for several months. In LNWR days, the shed was coded 8C, from 1935 to 1950 it was coded 2F, and ended its life with the code 2D. A little over four years before closure, its allocation reflected the nature of the traffic for which the shed provided motive power:

Ex-LMS 'Ivatt' class 2 2–6–0	46445, 46446
Ex-LNWR 7F 0–8–0	49330, 49415, 49425, 49441, 49442, 49446
Ex-MR 'Johnson' class 2 0–6–0	58217, 58278, 58293, 58306
	Total: 12

Running off Coventry shed in August 1952 is ex-LNWR 7F 0–8–0, BR no. 49414, very much the type of heavy freight engine for which Coventry shed was known.

An early twentieth-century view of the L&B station at Rugby. This was the final station, built by the LNWR in 1886. Like Coventry, the L&B provided inadequate facilities at Rugby when the line opened in 1838. This was highlighted as Rugby became a junction with the opening of the Midland Counties Railway whose line ran from Nottingham and Derby to Leicester, with an extension to Rugby being completed on 30 June 1840. A new station became necessary with the opening of the MCR, and an Act giving Royal Assent for the new facility was passed in 1848. By 1851, more lines entered Rugby, including the Trent Valley Railway, opened in 1848, a line from Market Harborough in 1850, and a local line from Leamington which opened in 1851. By 1881, a completely new station was required at Rugby, the structure seen in this photograph, which still stands today. This station consists of a large island platform and bays were provided at each end. The island was big enough to handle two main line trains at a time, scissor crossings providing independent paths of approach.

Ex-LNWR 'Precedent' class 2–4–0 with LMS no. 5000 (LNWR no. 2190) *Princess Beatrice* waits at the coaling stage of Rugby locoshed in February 1932. A shed was placed here in L&B days and two new sheds (one for the Northern Division and the other for the Southern Division) were opened in 1853. By 1866, two large straight sheds had replaced those built in 1853. In LMS and BR days the shed was coded 2A until 8 September 1963. From 9 September, it was coded 1F until closure to steam on 25 May 1965. Its allocation of January 1957 was as follows:

Ex-LMS 'Compound' 4P 4–4–0	41105, 41113, 41122, 41162, 41165, 41172
Ex-LMS class 2 2–6–2T	41214, 41278
Ex-LMS class 4 2–6–4T	42061, 42062, 42489, 42541, 42573, 42576, 42577, 42585, 42615, 42669, 42673
Ex-LMS 4F 0–6–0	44064, 44395
Ex-LMS 'Black Five' 4–6–0	44711, 44712, 44715, 44716, 44831, 44833, 44836, 44837, 44860, 44862, 44863, 44866, 44867, 44870, 44903, 44915, 45419, 45493
Ex-LMS 'Jinty' 3F 0–6–0T	47269, 47677
Ex-LMS 8F 2–8–0	48085, 48173, 48427, 48437, 48559, 48757
Ex-LNWR 7F 0–8–0	48914, 49049, 49114, 49245, 49249, 49377, 49397, 49405, 49413, 49417, 49433, 49435, 49452
Ex-'MR' class 2F 0–6–0	58181, 58218, 58308

Total: 63

Ex-LNWR 'Precursor' class 4–4–0 and LMS, no. 5300 (LNWR no. 1617) *Hydra* at Rugby shed in 1933. In LNWR days, the shed was coded No. 8 and was described as 'very extensive' with an allocation of about 160 locos in 1909, which included no fewer than twenty-six of the then new 'Precursor' class locos. At that time, the shed employed nearly 900 men and there were sub-sheds at Warwick, Coventry, Peterborough, Stamford, Seaton and Market Harborough. Thus, Rugby shed was one of the largest and most important on the whole of the LNWR system.

Ex-Midland Railway 2F 0–6–0 no. 3891 stands at the side of Rugby shed on 27 August 1938. These locos were taken into the shed's stock from the small Midland Railway shed at the west end of Rugby station and from the sub-shed at Peterborough at the 1923 'Grouping'. MR types were to remain at Rugby until the late 1950s.

Ex-LMS 'Compound' 4P 4–4–0 no. 41122 outside Rugby shed on 11 April 1954. In view is the northlight pattern roof fitted to both sheds in 1866.

Ex-Midland Railway 0–6–0 no. 52465 in use as a stationary boiler at Rugby shed on 11 April 1954.

Rugby shed was a supplier of heavy freight locos in the 1950s, and included in its allocation were several ex-LNWR 7F 0–8–0 tender engines for such work, along with some ex-LMS Stanier 8F 2–8–0s. Here, a 7F, BR no. 48914, is seen outside Rugby shed on 11 April 1954.

Another ex-LNWR 7F, BR no. 49112, is seen outside Rugby shed on the same day. When Rugby shed was closed to steam in May 1965 its final allocation was made up of ten ex-LMS 'Black Five' 4–6–0s and five ex-LMS Stanier 8F 2–8–0s. In the early 1960s, as steam gave way to diesel-electric traction on top-link express trains, Rugby was given an allocation of ex-LMS 'Jubilee' class 4–6–0s and 'Princess-Royal' Pacifics.

Ex-LMS Stanier 'Princess-Royal' Pacific, no. 46206 *Princess Marie Louise* of Crewe North shed (5A) approaches Rugby station with a Glasgow-bound train. On leaving Rugby the train will traverse the Trent Valley Railway to Stafford, thereby avoiding Birmingham, and go on to Crewe. This view was probably taken at the end of the 1950s, and the loco was to become part of Rugby shed's allocation in 1961.

A timetable for 'The Midlander' express service which ran from Wolverhampton (High Level) to Euston, via Birmingham (New Street). This train ran along the whole of the L&B route from New Street.

Table 12

THE MIDLANDER
REFRESHMENT CAR EXPRESS
LONDON, BIRMINGHAM and WOLVERHAMPTON
WEEK DAYS
(Mondays to Fridays)

	am
Wolverhampton (High Level) .. ..dep	11D 0
Birmingham (New Street) .. .. „	11D30
Coventry .. .. „	11D56
	pm
London (Euston) .. .. arr	1 30
	pm
London (Euston) .. ..dep	5A50
Coventry .. ..arr	7 24
Birmingham (New Street) .. .. „	7 50
Bescot .. .. „	8 14
Wolverhampton (High Level) .. .. „	8 30

A—Seats can be reserved in advance on payment of a fee of 1s. 0d. per seat (see page 26).

D—Except for 26th July, 1st, 2nd, 5th, 6th and 9th August, seats can be reserved in advance on payment of a fee of 1s. 0d. per seat (see page 26).

Bushbury (3B), Wolverhampton-based ex-LMS Stanier 'Jubilee' class 4–6–0 no. 45738 *Samson* leaves Rugby for Euston with the 11.50 a.m. Wolverhampton–Euston express on a summer Saturday. These engines were regularly used on these trains, having replaced LMS 'Compound' 4P 4–4–0s in the 1940s.

THE TRENT
VALLEY RAILWAY

Almost as soon as the L&B and GJR opened, proposals were put forward for a route that would bypass the increasingly congested Birmingham area. This would eventually lead to the construction of the Trent Valley Railway. First, plans were made by the Manchester and Birmingham Railway for a line, via Stoke-on-Trent and Nuneaton, to Rugby which threatened to take traffic from the GJR. Following this, the independent Trent Valley Railway Company, based at Nuneaton, proposed a route from Stafford to Rugby. This interested the L&B, as it would make it independent of the GJR and avoid Birmingham altogether. The Euston company sought, and obtained, running powers over the new line.

Alarmed by a potential loss of traffic, Secretary of the GJR, Captain Mark Huish, set upon a plan to bring the M&B and L&B to the negotiating table. To bring this about, he sought an agreement with the GWR which would bring the broad gauge into Rugby, Birmingham, and even Liverpool. The GWR were, however, unaware of Huish's real motives and, after some consideration, the Paddington company agreed to join forces with the GJR. So alarmed were the L&B, who were very much against the broad gauge, that they sought talks with the GJR. In the end, the GJR financed the construction of the TVR in exchange for running powers. Thus, there was no further need for an alliance with the GWR and Captain Huish abandoned his agreement with them. Worse was to follow, as far as the GWR was concerned, as Huish became as obstructive as he could possibly be to the Paddington company's efforts to bring their own main line into Birmingham from London.

The construction of the TVR received Royal Assent on 21 July 1845, and the line was purchased jointly by the GJR, L&B and M&B in April 1846. Improved relations between the three former protagonists led to the formation of the mighty London and North Western Railway a few months later, with Captain Huish as General Manager. Thus, when the TVR opened on 15 September 1847, it was part of the new company and almost immediately became the direct route between Euston and the north-west of England. The L&B now carried only trains for Coventry, Birmingham and Wolverhampton.

Since opening, the most famous LNWR, LMS and BR (LM region) express trains between Scotland, North Wales, the north-west of England and Euston have run along the TVR, considerably shortening journey times between the north and the capital. Only the section between Rugby and Polesworth is in Warwickshire, the remaining section, from Tamworth to Stafford, is in Staffordshire. Like the L&B, the TVR remains open and is still the main route to Euston. It was electrified along with the L&B in the 1960s.

The remains of Bulkington station buildings, complete with LNWR nameboard, as they appeared in the early 1960s. The station was opened with the TVR and was originally named Stretton. It was destined to have a very short life, closing in 1931.

Shilton station as it appeared in LMS days, looking from the road overbridge above. The station was situated 6 miles south of Nuneaton and it came into use on 1 December 1847. As the station only served a small community, its passenger service was very sparse.

Shilton station in LNWR days. Access to the platform was from the road above, the booking office being situated by the roadside. The staircases and rear of the booking office can be seen in this view. None of the station buildings was particularly elegant, and by the 1950s the station had a very dilapidated appearance. Interestingly, although the booking office was brick-built, it was backed with timber, as can be seen here. This timber was patched up over the years and became very shabby later on.

Shilton station from the goods siding. The situation was provided with a siding from new, on the Down side, which was extended in 1898. The station closed to passengers on 16 September 1957 but survived for goods traffic until 1965.

Nuneaton station in LNWR days, with one of the company's tank locos at the far end of the platform. Although Nuneaton was provided with its own station when the TVR opened, it was only considered suitable for second-class status, the company placing greater emphasis on the status of Atherstone, Tamworth and Lichfield, which were all first-class stations. Yet Nuneaton was to grow into the largest of five junctions on the TVR, receiving a second line from Coventry in 1850 and lines from Hinckley in 1862, Leicester in 1864 and Moira in 1873. Such was the growing importance of Nuneaton that the station was enlarged and partly rebuilt in 1909. Refreshment facilities were not provided at Nuneaton until 1881, at a time when Anglo-Scottish expresses made refreshment stops here, as well as at Rugby, Stafford and Crewe. All of these places provided luncheon baskets, which for 3s contained half a chicken, with ham or tongue, or a portion of cold beef, salad, ice, bread, cheese and butter with either half a bottle of claret, two glasses of sherry or a pint of stout. In 1916, Nuneaton's importance as a refreshment stop was enhanced by major improvements when new drinking rooms were opened which provided breakfast, luncheon, tea, dinner and light refreshments.

Nuneaton station on 12 May 1937 with a diesel railcar departing from the platform. In the 1930s, the LMS experimented with diesel traction as a way of reducing costs at a time when the Great Depression was taking its toll on railway revenues. Seen here is one of the three 200 h.p. English-Electric built diesel-electric railcars operated by the LMS.

On 11 September 1954, ex-LMS 'Jubilee' class 4–6–0 no. 45584 *North-West Frontier* is seen passing Ashby Junction, Nuneaton at the head of a Manchester (London Road)–Euston express. This train had joined the TVR at Colwich, having run via Stoke-on-Trent.

Ex-LNWR 'B' class four cylinder 0–8–0 no. 1282 is seen at Nuneaton shed in about 1925. The LNWR built a shed at Nuneaton in 1878 on the fork between the line from Coventry and the TVR. This shed was doubled in size in 1888 and enlarged again in 1897. It was coded No. 4 in LNWR days, recoded 2D under LMS auspices in 1935, became 2B after nationalization, and finished its life as 5E from September 1963. The shed closed on 6 June 1966, ex-LMS 8F no. 48264 being the last loco off shed two days earlier. It was later demolished and no trace of it now remains. The shed provided freight locos and engines for local passenger work, as its allocation for January 1957 shows:

Ex-LMS 'Fowler' class 3 2–6–2T	40049
Ex-LMS 'Stanier' class 3 2–6–2T	40087, 40104, 40122, 40136, 40138, 40156, 40157, 40204, 40207
Ex-LMS class 2 2–6–2T	41226, 41322, 41323
Ex-LMS Hughes-Fowler Crab 2–6–0	42781, 42783, 42817, 42854, 42891
Ex-LMS class 4 2–6–0	43002, 43003, 43011, 43023, 43034
Ex-MR 3F 0–6–0	43308, 43786
Ex-LMS 4F 0–6–0	44157, 44292
Ex-LMS 3F Jinty 0–6–0T	47285, 47286, 47492, 47594
Ex-LMS Stanier 8F 2–8–0	48016, 48020, 48077, 48154, 48258, 48312, 48320, 48343, 48345, 48372, 48398, 48435, 48449, 48456, 48526, 48658, 48686, 48716, 48723, 48751
Ex-LNWR 7F 0–8–0	48927, 49002, 49068, 49112, 49120, 49142, 49172, 49181, 49293, 49314, 49342, 49350, 49414, 49430, 49432
Ex-L&Y 3F 0–6–0	52201
Ex-MR 2F 0–6–0	58118
	Total: 68

One of Nuneaton shed's allocation of ex-LMS 'Stanier' class 3 2–6–2 tank locos, no. 40207, stands in the shed yard on 1 November 1959.

Nuneaton shed was well known for its allocation of ex-LNWR 7F 0–8–0s, one of which, no. 49415, is seen outside the shed on 1 November 1959. The last of these engines left in 1962, having been transferred to Springs Branch locoshed.

Ex-LMS Jinty 0–6–0 tank loco no. 47594 is seen at Nuneaton shed on 4 July 1952. In its later life, Nuneaton shed took on an important role when, in 1965, it played host to Stanier 'Princess-Coronation' class Pacific no. 46235 *City of Birmingham*, when she went into storage before going on to be preserved at Birmingham Museum of Science and Industry.

Atherstone station in LNWR days with the Irish Mail passing through. This picture was taken before the line was quadrupled in 1901.

A view of Atherstone station shortly after the 1901 quadrupling. Atherstone was opened in 1847 as one of the first-class stations, no doubt because it served the gentry living close by in places like Merevale, Atherstone, Sheepy, Gapsall Halls and Cliffe House. The station was designed by J.W. Livock in the Jacobean (or Elizabethan) style, with steeply pitched roofs, tall patterned chimneys and alternating bands of patterned slates. The interior was altered and modernized at the same time as the line was quadrupled, but the frontage was little changed. In later years, the chimneys over the living accommodation were replaced by smaller, more modern ones. One unique feature of the station, after quadrupling, was the signal-box, which was placed centrally and carried on girders, as seen in this view. This new box replaced the original which was situated on the old Down platform, itself swept away during quadrupling. The new box, of timber construction, had its supports on the new Down platform and the slightly enlarged 'six foot'. Access to the box was via a catwalk from the Down side. One effect of this quadrupling was that it rid the LNWR of the problem of crossing a road, via a level-crossing, which had brought the company into dispute with Warwickshire County Council, who obtained a court injunction to prevent trains running over the level-crossing at more than 4 m.p.h. An Act passed in 1902 allowed the Euston company to divert and carry the road (Watling Street) over the railway and Coventry Canal by means of a bridge, and to close the level-crossing. At electrification, the unusual signal-box disappeared but the main building survives after years of threatened demolition, thanks to a partnership of private businesses and local government which assured its survival for use as office premises. Passengers, however, are forced to use 'bus-stop'-type waiting shelters now placed on the platforms.

Although in Staffordshire, Tamworth (another of the TVR first-class stations) is included here because it is right on the border between Warwickshire and Staffordshire. In fact, an LMS guide to the Irish Mail has the county boundary just beyond the platforms at the Stafford end. Here, ex-LNWR 'Jumbo' 2–4–0 no. 2194 *Cambrian* is seen at the head of a Down semi-fast train at Tamworth in 1925. Like Atherstone, Tamworth station's main building was built in the Jacobean style.

Leaving Tamworth with a Stafford-bound local train is ex-LMS 2P 4–4–0 no. 40652, actually in Staffordshire. In the background, the Midland Railway's Birmingham and Derby Junction line can be seen crossing the TVR.

LNWR BRANCHES

Following the opening of the L&B, the company began to develop a branch from Coventry to Leamington Spa, the town being a well-known 'watering place' and resort. In 1842, the Euston company supported the formation of the Warwick and Leamington Railway, its line opening in December 1844. It ran from Coventry to a station at Milverton, near Warwick. The company was more keen on advertising the spa than the historic castle town of Warwick, so the station was known as Leamington (Milverton). The line had one intermediate station at Kenilworth.

After the L&B had become part of the LNWR, Leamington was regarded as something of a frontier town, a place where any opposing railway should be prevented from entering. The opposition was the Great Western Railway, whose route from Oxford to Birmingham was planned to pass through the town. As the LNWR was already established here, it used its presence as an excuse to make the GWR lay mixed gauge tracks all the way from Leamington to Birmingham, in its efforts to frustrate the Paddington company.

The L&B had been forced to admit that its line from Euston to Birmingham, via Coventry, was rather circuitous but, they argued, it would still be shorter than the proposed GWR route, then supported by the GJR, which was to run via Oxford and Rugby. However, the possible threat of competition from Paddington was met when the new LNWR extended its line from Milverton right into Leamington, and then built a branch from there to Rugby. The Milverton to Leamington extension was authorized in 1846 using a Bill originally proposed by the L&B. The branch to Rugby was awarded to the Rugby and Leamington Railway, whose line ran from Rugby to Leamington Priors (later to become Avenue) station. Doubts were raised about the profitability of the line and, by September 1848, the LNWR board considered abandoning the route. Work was restarted, however, in 1850 after a deputation was sent from Warwick to Euston in order to lobby local MPs. The single line was finally completed in 1851. One other line which ran into Leamington was the branch from Weedon, opened in 1895.

As the GWR completed its own route from Paddington, via Oxford and Leamington, to Birmingham (Snow Hill), there was speculation that it might seek running powers to Coventry, very much an LNWR stronghold, after the completion of a spur with the Euston company at Leamington in 1864. Such powers were never actually sought, not least because the line from Leamington to Coventry was single and the LNWR refused to double it for that reason. However, the section between Kenilworth Junction and Milverton was doubled some twenty years later, but this was only because extra traffic was generated with the opening of a 'cut-off' route between Kenilworth Junction and Berkswell, on the L&B main line, in 1884.

The branch from Leamington to Weedon closed to passengers in 1959. The Leamington–Coventry line itself closed to passengers in 1965, only to be reopened to the ex-GWR Leamington station in 1966. Trains from Birmingham (New Street) to the south coast resorts use this route since Birmingham (Snow Hill) closed to express traffic in March 1967.

Leamington (Milverton) station, actually in Warwick, was on a branch from the L&B at Coventry. The station was the terminus of the Warwick and Leamington Union Railway, formed in 1842. The line opened in December 1844, under L&B control. In those days, Leamington was a very important spa town and the railway company preferred to use the spa town's name, considering it more important than historic Warwick.

Another view of Milverton station. In LNWR days, a line from Rugby ran to Milverton (and Leamington) but it was not considered important, offering only a shorter route to Warwick than that offered by its rival, the GWR. A line from Northampton also ran to Milverton. Rationalization, under the Beeching plan, spelt the end for Milverton; it closed to goods on 4 January 1965 and to passengers six days later.

An important station for the LNWR was Leamington Spa Avenue and it is seen here at the turn of the century. The station was called Leamington Priors when it first opened in 1844, and underwent several name changes until it finally became Leamington Spa Avenue. The last line to reach Leamington, via Milverton, was the Weedon Branch which opened in 1895. It was, incidentally, the first to close to passengers in 1958. The LMS considered its branches around Leamington important enough to house some top-link locos at nearby Warwick shed, including ex-LNWR 'Experiment' class 4–6–0s and 'Precursor' class 4–4–0s, in 1928. Local services were, however, in the hands of LNWR 2–4–2 tank locos, later replaced by Ivatt 2–6–2 tanks on Nuneaton–Leamington services. In the 1930s, the first pneumatic tyred railcars, built by Armstrong Siddeley of Coventry, were used on Coventry–Leamington lines. These cars were powered by a V12 engine and could reach speeds of up to 75 m.p.h.

le 73 NORTHAMPTON, BLISWORTH, WEEDON, DAVENTRY AND LEAMINGTON SPA

		SX	SO		a.m.	a.m.	a.m.	a.m.	a.m.	p.m.	p.m.	SO	p.m.	p.m.	p.m.	p.m.	p.m.	p.m.	SO	
Miles		a.m.	a.m.	a.m.								p.m.	p.m.						p.m.	
	London (Euston) .... dep.	...	...	...	...	...	...	...	...	...	...	...	...	12 20	...	4 35	...	7 5	...	7 30	...
0	**Northampton** (Castle) ...dep.	6 57	7 10	.	8 25	8 45	9 0	9 52	11 2	12 17	1 30	...	2 32	...	4 23	5 30	6 14	7 12	8 48	9 30	10 0	...
4¾	Blisworth .... { arr.	7 7	7 20	...	8 35	8 56	9 10	10 2	11 12	12 27	1 40	...	2 45	...	4 33	5 40	6 24	7 22	8 58	9 40	10 10	...
	{ dep.	.	.	...	8 55	.	.	.	.	.	.	...	...	...	4 40	...	6 35	...	9 11	.	.	...
11¾	**Weedon** ....dep.	...	...	...	9A19	...	...	...	...	...	...	...	...	4851	...	...	6 46	...	9 24	...	...	...
	Daventry .... { arr.	.	.	...	9 28	...	...	...	...	...	...	...	...	5 0	...	...	6 55	...	9 33	...	...	...
15¾	{ dep.	.	.	...	9 31	...	...	...	...	...	...	...	...	5 3	...	...	7 14	...	9 36	...	...	...
19	Braunston	.	.	...	9 39	...	...	...	...	...	...	...	...	5 14	...	...	7 21	...	9 42	...	...	...
21¼	Flecknoe	.	.	...	9 46	...	...	...	...	...	...	...	...	5 20	...	...	...	...	9 48	...	...	...
25	Napton & Stockton	.	.	8 12	9 53	...	...	...	...	...	.	1 43	...	5 13	5 27	...	...	7 33	...	9 55	...	...
27	Southam & Long I.	.	.	8 18	9 59	...	...	...	...	...	.	1 48	...	5 18	5 35	...	...	7 39	...	10 2	...	...
34¾	**Leamington Spa** ... arr.	.	.	8 35	10 16	...	...	...	...	...	.	2 5	...	5 35	5 52	...	...	7 56	...	10 20	...	...
35	Warwick (Milverton) .... "	.	.	8 57	10 38	...	...	...	...	...	.	2 23	...	5 50	6 15	...	...	8 21	...	10 25	...	...

† —a.m.   **A**—Arrive Weedon 9.5 a.m.   **SX**—Saturdays excepted.

SO—Saturdays only.

A timetable for services over the Weedon branch to Northampton and Leamington/Milverton in the 1950s, only a few years before its closure.

Leamington Spa Avenue station in LMS days, with a local train at the platform. The station was provided with a through service from Euston, to compete with the GWR whose main line between Paddington and Birmingham (Snow Hill) served the town. A slip coach was used from Rugby (and Weedon at one time) until 1932.

A deserted Leamington Avenue station. Services from Rugby ceased in 1959, but services from Coventry lasted until 1965. The station finally closed to passengers on 18 January 1965 and to goods on 19 May 1969. The Coventry–Leamington line itself was reopened in May 1977 and some Birmingham–Solihull–Leamington Inter-City services were diverted to serve Coventry and Birmingham International, for the airport and National Exhibition Centre.

Kenilworth station, on the line between Leamington and Coventry. When the Warwick and Leamington Union Railway was opened in 1844, Kenilworth was the only intermediate station on the route. In 1851, the GWR had completed its main line from Paddington to Birmingham and there were fears that the Paddington company might seek running powers into the LNWR stronghold at Coventry. To prevent this happening, the LNWR refused to double the line all the way to Coventry. As it transpired, the GWR was not interested in reaching Coventry. The section between Kenilworth Junction and Milverton was doubled some twenty years later because extra traffic had been generated following the opening of a cut-off between Kenilworth and Berkswell, on the L&B main line, in 1884.

Kenilworth station as it appeared in the 1950s. The station closed to passengers on 18 January 1965, but the line through this well-heeled town has been given a new lease of life as the Inter-City route between Coventry and the old GWR main line at Leamington, although the line is single and no station actually exists at Kenilworth.

Running along the line between Kenilworth Junction and Berkswell in the early 1950s is ex-LMS Fairburn 2–6–4 tank no. 42182 with a three coach local train.

Ex-LMS Fowler 4F 2–6–4 tank loco no. 42309 heads a three coach local train through Foleshill, on the Coventry–Bedworth line, in 1960.

Coundon Road station, on the Coventry–Nuneaton line, as it appeared on 23 August 1981. The line between Coventry and Nuneaton was opened in 1850 and remains in use today.

The signal-box at Coundon Road station.

Another view of Coundon Road signal-box.

Hawkesbury Lane signal-box as it appeared on 10 February 1984 with Class 31 loco no. 31.260 on a ballast train to Banbury.

Hawkesbury Lane station as it appeared on 13 June 1966, complete with main station building and wooden waiting shelter.

The small signal cabin at Bedlam Crossing on 14 October 1983 with signalman Bob Barnes on the steps.

The signal-box at Nuneaton Midland Junction with the 1400 Sprinter set no. 150.125 being stopped by signalman Bob Barnes because no lights were showing. This picture was taken on 15 July 1988.

THE GREAT WESTERN RAILWAY MAIN LINE

Competition with the LNWR for traffic between Birmingham and London became an established fact when the GWR opened its own main line from Oxford, where it left the existing route from Paddington, to Birmingham (Snow Hill) on Friday 1 October 1852. This new route had a difficult gestation and birth, thanks to the efforts of Captain Mark Huish, the autocratic General Manager of the LNWR, who resorted to every tactic, both legal and illegal, either to prevent construction or to make progress as difficult as he possibly could.

When Captain Huish abandoned the GWR, after reaching an agreement with the L&B over their dispute concerning the Trent Valley Railway, the Paddington company supported the Birmingham and Oxford Junction Railway's plan to build a broad gauge line between Oxford and Birmingham. The line was authorized on 3 August 1946, with a capital of £1 million in £20 shares.

The original Bill of 1845 allowed for sale or lease to the GWR, a move that Huish tried to prevent by buying up some 40,000 shares in the B&OJ in 1846, many costing £11 each (way above their true value) to try and gain a controlling interest and bring the line into the LNWR empire. He even went as far as attempting to gain a majority of directors on the B&OJ board, which he failed to do. This failure forced Huish to resort to illegal tactics, when he forged the B&OJ company seal, declaring it to be the 'only common seal of the B&OJ'. With this seal, a 'planted' board made an agreement for the LNWR to acquire the line. Alarmed by Huish's activities, the GWR went to court and won, the B&OJ finally becoming part of the Paddington company in August 1847.

Undeterred by their defeat in the courts, the LNWR was still prepared to be difficult rather than quietly withdraw, and followed a policy of being as obstructive as possible. Firstly, the Euston company insisted on having running powers at Banbury (Oxon), forcing the GWR to lay mixed gauge tracks. Then, the LNWR insisted on a clause in the B&OJ Act that would make it unlawful for the GWR to use the authorized broad gauge until they had completed and opened a link between the B&OJ and the LNWR in Birmingham, or within 1 mile thereof, by means of a double line of narrow gauge rails. Running powers were never exercised and these tracks were only inserted to make life as difficult as possible for the GWR.

As construction of the B&OJ progressed, the question of a junction with the LNWR in Birmingham needed to be addressed. After much argument, it was agreed that a viaduct carrying a narrow gauge branch from Bordesley to Curzon Street would be constructed. When the Duddeston Viaduct reached LNWR land, building stopped, never to restart, and the line was never laid, neither company actually wanting it. On leaving Birmingham (Moor Street) station, this 'white elephant' viaduct can be seen on the left as trains run towards Bordesley station, a monument to LNWR bloody-mindedness against a rival company that was prepared to take them on and win. The LNWR insisted that the B&OJ also had to be mixed gauge between Leamington and Birmingham so that it could have access to the route, for no other reason than to make construction more expensive and difficult than it need have been.

When the B&OJ finally opened, the new line operated trains between Paddington and Birmingham using broad gauge 2–2–2 and 4–2–2 locos, services timed to cover the whole route in about three hours. It would not be until the early twentieth century that the GWR would compete with the LNWR on distance and timing.

Fenny Compton station on the B&OJ, second station from Oxford on the line from Paddington to Birmingham (Snow Hill). This was one of the original stations when the GWR line opened in 1850.

Another view of Fenny Compton station as it appeared in the 1950s. By the time this view was taken, the goods yard had become somewhat overgrown, having closed in 1958. The station itself closed to passengers on 2 November 1964.

Southam Road and Harbury station was another of the original B&OJ stations. It is seen here in the 1950s, showing a rather modern footbridge.

Another view of Southam Road and Harbury station. The station closed to goods traffic on 11 November 1963 and to passengers on 2 November 1964.

Ex-GWR 2–6–3 prairie tank loco no. 5170 runs light past Leamington East Junction signal-box on its way to the station in the 1950s. Another of the original B&OJ stations, it was to be the centre of celebrations for the opening of the new line, with a banquet held at the Royal Hotel. Things, however, did not go well as the train bringing guests to Leamington for the event, headed by broad gauge loco *Lord of the Isles* was involved in an accident when it ran into the back of a goods train, running late, at Aynho. In the event, the celebrations went ahead when guests were brought late to Leamington and sat down to their celebration meal at 4 p.m. The train had been scheduled to run all the way to Birmingham, but never made it. The original Leamington station was demolished and replaced by a modern structure in the late 1930s. This station is still in use, although goods services were closed on 19 May 1969.

Ex-GWR 2–6–2 prairie tank loco no. 4112 is being loaded with coal at Leamington locoshed in 1958.

A general view of Leamington locoshed in GWR days, showing the main shed building and coaling stage with water tank above. In view are a pair of prairie tanks and loco coal wagons. With the opening of the B&OJ, the GWR began operating local services from Leamington Spa to Birmingham. This would become important when Birmingham businessmen moved out of the city and into more rural areas towards the end of the nineteenth century, commuting to the city centre every day and to Stratford-upon-Avon, via Hatton Junction. To supply locos for these services, the GWR provided a wooden shed which survived until it burned down in 1902. A replacement shed was opened in September 1906, the one shown here. The shed was allocated thirty locos but the number fell to as low as nineteen in 1954, as the allocation below shows:

Collett 0–6–0PT	3619, 3624, 3631, 7702
Collett 0–6–2T	6624, 6657, 6697
Churchward 2–6–2T	4112, 4171, 5104, 5161, 5184, 5185, 5192, 5194
Collett 2–6–2T	8100, 8109
'Austerity' 2–8–0	90466, 90563
	Total: 19

Most of the allocation were tank locos for suburban passenger train use. In 1958, Western Region took control of the old LNWR line to Leamington Avenue and the old LNWR shed at Warwick was closed on 17 November 1958. Its allocation of four Ivatt 2–6–2 tank locos and one 8F 2–8–0 was transferred to the GWR shed. Leamington shed, coded LMTN in GWR days and 84D in BR days, closed in June 1965, after services on the GWR line had changed to diesel.

Ex-GWR Hawksworth designed 0–6–0 pannier tank no. 9475, shunts wagons outside Warwick station in the 1950s.

Table 13

CAMBRIAN COAST EXPRESS
LONDON, ABERDOVEY, TOWYN,
BARMOUTH, PWLLHELI and ABERYSTWYTH

WEEK DAYS

		R E am	R S am				R S am	R E am
London (Paddington)	..dep	10A10	10A50	Aberystwyth	..dep	9A25		11A1
			pm	Borth	.. .. ,,	9A45		11A3
Banbury General ..	{arr	11 20	12 11	Dovey Junction	..arr	10 0		11 5
	{dep	11 22	12 15					
Leamington Spa	{arr	..	12 39	Pwllheli ..	..dep	..		9A3
General	{dep	..	12 43	Criccieth	.. .. ,,	..		9A4
		pm		Portmadoc	.. .. ,,	..		10A
Birmingham	{arr	12 13	1 15	Harlech ..	.. .. ,,	..		10A2
(Snow Hill)	{dep	12 17	1 20	Barmouth..	.. .. ,,	..		10A5
Wolverhampton	{arr	12 37	1 39	Barmouth Junction..	.. ,,	8A45		11A
(Low Level)	{dep	12 44	1 46	Fairbourne	.. .. ,,	8A50		11A
Shrewsbury	{arr	1 19	..	Llwyngwril	.. .. ,,	9A 5		11A1
	{dep	1 23	..	Tonfanau	.. .. ,,	9 15		11 2
Welshpool	..arr	2 1	2 56	Towyn ..	.. .. ,,	9A22		11A3
Newtown	.. ,,	2 30	3 28	Aberdovey	.. .. ,,	9A30		11A3
Machynlleth ..	.. .. ,,	3 17	4 18	Penhelig Halt ..	.. ,,	9 36		11 4
				Dovey Junction	..arr	9 50		11 5
Machynlleth ..	..dep	3 40	4 30					
Penhelig Halt ..	..arr	4 4	4 51					
Aberdovey ..	.. .. ,,	4 10	4 56	Dovey Junction ..	..dep	10A 8		12A
Towyn ..	.. .. ,,	4 19	5 3	Machynlleth	.. .. ,,	10A20		12A1
Llwyngwril ..	.. .. ,,	4 36	5 15	Newtown ..	.. .. ,,	11 17		1 2
Fairbourne ..	.. .. ,,	4 46	5 24	Welshpool ..	.. .. ,,	11 55		1 5
Barmouth Junction ..	.. ,,	4 50	5 27	Shrewsbury ..	{arr	..		2 3
Barmouth ..	.. .. ,,	4 57	5 33		{dep	..		2 4
Harlech ..	.. .. ,,	5 30	6 0			pm		
Portmadoc..	.. .. ,,	5 54	6 21	Wolverhampton	{arr	1 11		3 2
Criccieth ..	.. .. ,,	6 10	6 35	(Low Level)	{dep	1 18		3 3
Pwllheli ..	.. .. ,,	6 26	7 0	Birmingham	{arr	1 38		3 5
				(Snow Hill)	{dep	1 42		4
Machynlleth ..	..dep	3 22	4 23	Leamington Spa	{arr	2 11		4 2
Borth	..arr	3 45	4 46	General	{dep	2 13		4 2
Aberystwyth ..	.. .. ,,	4 5	5 10	London (Paddington)	..arr	4 10		6 .

A—Seats can be reserved in advance on payment of a fee of 1s. 0d. per seat (see page 26).
E—Except Saturdays
R—Refreshment Car facilities between Paddington and Aberystwyth
S—Saturdays only

A timetable for the Cambrian Coast Express which ran from Paddington to Aberystwyth/Pwllheli on the Welsh Cambrian Coast, via the B&OJ.

Warwick station as it appeared in Western Region days. The GWR recognized the importance of this historic county town with its famous castle and a station was opened here with the start of B&OJ operations. The town now features in the BBC police/medical drama, 'Dangerfield'.

Another view of Warwick station in the 1950s. The station remains open, but goods facilities closed here on 31 January 1969.

After leaving Warwick, the B&OJ climbs the famous Hatton Bank, which runs for 3¼ miles at 1 in 110 before arriving at Hatton Station. Hatton is the junction for the branch to Stratford-upon-Avon, which once continued on to Bristol. Hatton station is seen here, looking towards Birmingham, on 13 September 1956.

Hatton station, again looking towards Birmingham, in 1956. The station nameboard requests that passengers for Stratford-upon-Avon change here.

Approaching Hatton with a Down goods train is ex-GWR Collett 'Hall' class 4–6–0 no. 5945 *Leckhampton Hall* in 1956. Hatton is still in use as a station, but goods facilities were closed here on 11 November 1963.

A 1950s timetable for the Inter-City which ran between Wolverhampton (Low Level) and Paddington, via Birmingham (Snow Hill), and along the B&OJ.

THE INTER-CITY

REFRESHMENT CAR EXPRESS

LONDON, BIRMINGHAM and WOLVERHAMPTON

WEEK DAYS
(Mondays to Fridays)

	am
London (Paddington) .. ..dep	9 A 0
High Wycombe .. .. „	9 K 31
Birmingham (Snow Hill) .. ..arr	11 7
Wolverhampton (Low Level) .. .. „	11 30

	pm
Wolverhampton (Low Level) .. ..dep	4 B 35
Birmingham (Snow Hill) .. .. „	5 B 0
Leamington Spa General .. .. „	5 26
High Wycombe .. ..arr	6 V 41
London (Paddington) .. .. „	7 15

A—Seats can be reserved in advance on payment of a fee of 1s. 0d. per seat (see page 26).

B—Except for 26th July and 2nd August, seats can be reserved in advance on payment of a fee of 1s. 0d. per seat (see page 26).

K—Calls to pick up passengers only.

V—Calls to set down passengers only.

The branch from Hatton to Stratford-upon-Avon was constructed as part of the B&OJ to join the Oxford, Worcester and Wolverhampton Railway's branch from Worcester to Stratford-upon-Avon. It was absorbed by the GWR on 31 August 1848 and opened on 1 October 1852. The first station from Hatton was at Claverdon, seen in this 1950s view that shows the simple station buildings.

The exterior of Claverdon station, showing the roadside booking office.

The GWR doubled the little branch in 1937 and Claverdon station was moved a few yards to the Bearley side of a road overbridge. The branch's status as a double line was short lived as it was singled again during the 1970s rationalization. The station was closed to goods traffic on 20 May 1963. Since rationalization, only a single platform with a simple waiting shelter remains, as seen in this 1980s view.

The next station on the little branch was at Bearley, seen here in the 1950s with the goods shed just visible on the left.

Bearley station, looking towards Bearley Junction, where it meets the Birmingham and North Warwickshire line before running to Stratford-upon-Avon. The branch was useful to the GWR, providing access to Stratford-upon-Avon from Paddington, Birmingham and Leamington. Its importance declined, however, when the B&NW opened, although locals serving Stratford from Leamington continued to use the line, and expresses could still run direct from Paddington. Indeed, during the 1920s and '30s, the GWR operated the 'Shakespeare Express' from Paddington to Stratford, via Leamington Spa, leaving at 9.25 a.m. Bearley station lost its goods siding on 20 May 1963, but the station remains open, as does Claverdon, providing local traffic between Stratford and Hatton, for connections to Leamington and Birmingham, via Solihull.

After leaving Bearley, a little branch left the Stratford-upon-Avon line to reach the Midland Railway at Alcester. It had one intermediate station at Great Alne, pictured here after closure in the 1930s.

The terminus of the branch was at Alcester. The Midland line from Broome Junction to Ashchurch also passed through Alcester, and the station appears to be of Midland design rather than GWR. The little branch closed after the Second World War.

After leaving Bearley, the Stratford line entered Wilmcote station, the village once being the home of William Shakespeare's mother, Mary Arden. Her home can still be seen at Wilmcote. The original station serving the village was closed on 8 December 1907 and replaced by this one when the new B&NW was opened. The attractive GWR footbridge provided at the new station can be seen here.

Another view of Wilmcote station, from the road above the railway. Note the bicycle shed on the Up platform. Wilmcote station remains open, serving the attractive little village, but its goods siding was closed on 11 November 1963.

The important station at Stratford-upon-Avon, which serves the famous home of playwright William Shakespeare and mecca for tourists from all over the world. As befits such an important destination, a large station was provided here, as can be seen, and is built in typical GWR style with the famous platform awnings. The station still plays an important role, although its goods services ceased on 6 May 1968. The station is also now a terminus, having lost its through line after Dr Beeching transferred all traffic to Bristol on to the Midland Railway main line from Birmingham (New Street), via the Lickey Bank, in September 1962.

The island platform at Stratford in the 1950s, showing the station buildings. The BR Western Region station nameboard is visible beyond the bridge.

Stratford-upon-Avon station looking towards Honeybourne in the 1950s.

The exterior and main entrance to the GWR station at Stratford-upon-Avon. Among the many adverts on the wall is a timetable for Midland Red buses which operated in the town.

A general view of Stratford-upon-Avon station with a steam railmotor train, probably from the North Warwickshire line, which has terminated here, and a rake of GWR coaches on the island platform.

Ex-GWR pannier tank 0–6–0 no. 3725 waits at Stratford-upon-Avon station with a two-coach Leamington train, some time in the 1950s.

Another 0–6–0 pannier tank, no. 9429, has just arrived at Stratford-upon-Avon with a train from Leamington Spa in the 1950s.

After leaving Stratford-upon-Avon, the line joined the Oxford, Worcester and Wolverhampton Railway's line for Worcester. After passing Racecourse Platform, which served Stratford racecourse, the line passed Milcote station. This view shows the second station, the first having closed on 9 May 1908. This second station was closed on 3 January 1966, when the whole route to Worcester and Bristol was terminated, having shut down to goods traffic on 1 July 1963.

From Milcote, the OW&W passed through Long Marston station, seen here in the 1950s.

Another view of Long Marston station, showing the station buildings and level-crossing. The station closed at the same time as Milcote, its goods siding having been closed on 7 September 1964.

Next station on the line was Pebworth Halt. This very simple station had only a wooden platform and crude shelter, as seen here. The station closed with the line. After leaving Pebworth Halt the line headed towards Honeybourne Junction in Worcestershire.

Back on the B&OJ, the next station after Hatton was at Lapworth, here showing the attractive GWR building. This picture was taken in GWR days, probably before the First World War. Note the advertisements on the station footbridge for something called 'Nectar Tea'. When, I wonder, did this brand disappear?

Another view of Lapworth station. In the years before the B&NW opened, passengers for Henley-in-Arden changed here.

A little GWR 0–4–2 tank waits at the old Henley-in-Arden station with its train from Rowington Junction, near Lapworth, *c*. 1900. Plans for a railway to Henley-in-Arden, a town famous for its ice-cream, dated from 28 June 1861, when a scheme had been projected to build a mixed gauge branch of just over 3 miles in length. Half of the line was constructed, but it remained semi-derelict until the route was completed, under GWR influence, on 6 June 1894 by the Birmingham and Henley-in-Arden Railway Company. The GWR absorbed them on 1 July 1900, only a month before the Paddington company took control of the B&NW company. Passenger services along the branch commenced at opening and survived until 1 January 1915. The B&NW opening, in 1908, made the little line superfluous to requirements. In 1917, the branch was totally closed and most of the track was lifted, the steel used in the war effort. Only the stub connecting the B&NW station at Henley-in-Arden with the goods yard at the old Henley station remained *in situ*, the goods yard being used by the B&NW.

The goods yard at the old Henley-in-Arden station after closure in June 1965. The former passenger station is visible in the distance.

The old Henley-in-Arden station as it appeared in 1965, after it had closed to goods traffic.

The former passenger station building at Henley-in-Arden (old station) in 1965.

The goods shed at Henley-in-Arden old station in 1965.

An interesting view here, of the locoshed that had been in use when the branch from Rowington to Henley was to open. This view was taken in 1965, but the locoshed had closed fifty years earlier when the little branch had shut down. It only survived because it was used as a goods shed for the B&NW at Henley-in-Arden.

Another view of the derelict station at Henley-in-Arden.

After leaving Lapworth, the B&OJ heads towards the typical suburban station at Knowle and Dorridge. This station is still open and is important as a source of commuter traffic to and from Birmingham. Goods facilities, however, ceased here from 7 September 1964.

Predecessors of 'Star', 'Castle' and 'King' class 4–6–0s on Birmingham–Paddington expresses were 'Atbara' double-framed 4–4–0s one of which, no. 4147 *St John's*, is seen at the head of an express as it passes through Widney Manor station.

A view of Widney Manor station in the 1950s. The station remains open for commuter traffic, but it was closed to goods on 6 May 1963.

Another 'Atbara' 4–4–0, no. 4115, is seen passing Widney Manor with an express train.

A turn-of-the-century view of the substantial station at Solihull. This station was important as it served quite a large, well-heeled town. The station is still open today, but only the island platform remains, which is accessed through a subway from the road below.

Another view of Solihull station, with two locos waiting beyond the island platform. Also in view, behind the signal-box, is the goods siding. Goods facilities were withdrawn at Solihull on 6 July 1964.

GWR double-framed 4–4–0 no. 4162 waits at Olton station with a semi-fast train.

On the outer suburbs of Birmingham lies Acocks Green station, seen here in 1905 looking towards Olton. Approaching is GWR 0–4–2 tank loco of the '517' class, with a local train for Leamington. There appear to be several potential passengers awaiting the train's arrival and the Edwardian fashions of the day are clearly visible. This station was demolished when the section was widened from two to four tracks in 1906–7.

The new station at Acocks Green shortly after opening in 1907. Acocks Green was one of the original B&OJ stations which opened on 1 October 1852.

A view from under the canopy on the island platform at Acocks Green in the 1950s.

Acocks Green station shortly after rebuilding in 1907. The railway and station, like others in Birmingham, had to compete with Birmingham Corporation bus services which affected revenue. However, the station still survives but lost its goods facilities in the 1960s.

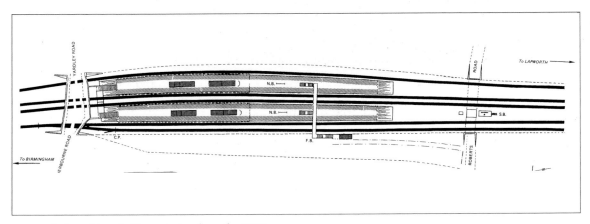

A plan of Acocks Green station from the 1930s.

A local train for Birmingham (Moor Street), headed by GWR 2–4–0 tank engine no. 1445, waits at Acocks Green station in 1910.

An 0–4–2 tank engine heads another Birmingham local during the same period.

Tyseley station, looking towards Acocks Green, in GWR days. The station at Tyseley was opened on 1 October 1906 to serve the B&OJ and B&NW, the latter opening in 1908 and making Tyseley an important junction. The station was provided with two island platforms, 520 ft long, with red brick buildings in which were waiting rooms, on both islands. Each of the islands was covered by standard GWR wooden canopies. Access was via the road above, which crossed the station at the Paddington end. The booking office was situated in the roadside building, passengers descending by separate staircases to the island platforms.

The Birmingham end of Tyseley station with the goods shed on the right and the locoshed in the distance on the left. Tyseley handled much freight traffic, including motor cycles produced at factories nearby.

Running through Tyseley with a fitted freight train from Birmingham is ex-LMS 'Black Five' 4–6–0 no. 44872.

A diesel parcels car runs through Tyseley and heads towards Acocks Green in October 1966.

A row of Wolverhampton-built GWR 0–6–0 pannier tanks, the centre one numbered 1947, at Tyseley locoshed road in 1930. Tyseley shed opened in June 1908, replacing a structure at Bordesley Junction built in 1855. Along with the shed, a maintenance factory was also established here. This plant undertook heavy repair work of GWR locos in the Birmingham area. This work actually ceased in 1931 when the factory was transferred to Wolverhampton Stafford Road. The works, however, still carried out some repair work until 1964.

Allocation at Tyseley for May 1954   Codes: GWR – TYS
BR – 84E became 2A from September 1963

Collett 0–6–0 PT 7438, 9753, 9798	3625, 3646, 3660, 3673, 3689, 3693, 3769, 4648, 5736, 5738, 5790, 7713, 7735, 7758, 8700, 9608, 9614, 9635, 9680, 9682, 9724, 9733,
Hawksworth 0–6–0PT	8415, 8417, 8468, 9432
Churchward 2–6–2T 5198	4110, 4111, 4116, 4170, 4172, 5152, 5156, 5163, 5164, 5166, 5181,
Collett 2–6–2T	3101, 6105, 6116, 6118, 6134, 6139, 6166,8108
Collett 0–6–2T	6614, 6620, 6668, 6669
Collett Goods 0–6–0	2238, 2257, 2279, 2296
Churchward 2–6–0 7317,	5322, 5333, 5369, 5370, 5386, 6307, 6321, 6327, 6336, 6342, 6394, 9303, 9319
Churchward 2–8–0	2826, 2848, 2849, 2856, 2867, 3829, 3839

Collett 'Hall' class 4–6–0	4964 *Rodwell Hall*	5900 *Hinderton Hall*
	5909 *Newton Hall*	5912 *Quenn's Hall*
	5927 *Guild Hall*	6904 *Charfield Hall*
Hawksworth 'Modified Hall' 4–6–0	6971 *Athelhampton Hall*	7912 *Little Linford Hall*
	7913 *Little Wyrley Hall*	7918 *Rhose Wood Hall*
	7929 *Wyke Hall*	
Collett 'Grange' class 4–6–0	6843 *Poulton Grange*	6853 *Morehampton Grange*
	6858 *Woolston Grange*	6866 *Morfa Grange*
Collett 'Manor' class 4–6–0	7818 *Granville Manor*	7821 *Ditcheat Manor*
Diesel shunters	13004, 13025, 13026, 13027, 13028, 13029	

TOTAL: Steam locos – 95, Diesels – 6: 101

Awaiting access to the goods yard at Small Heath, ex-GWR Churchward 2–6–0 no. 5386 rests with its goods train in July 1956.

Small Heath and Sparkbrook station as it appeared in the mid-1950s. The station has two island platforms, with red brick, flat-roofed station buildings covered by standard GWR wooden canopies. Access to the station is from Golden Hillock Road which runs across the railway at the Birmingham end. Nearby used to stand the famous BSA motor cycle works which 'went to the wall' in the early 1970s, sending shock waves throughout the whole of the motor industry in the West Midlands at that time. During the last war, the factory took a direct hit in the Blitz, causing great loss of life. From here, trains from the B&OJ headed towards Birmingham (Snow Hill), via Bordesley station.

THE NORTH WARWICKSHIRE RAILWAY

The Birmingham and North Warwickshire Railway, to give the line its full title, but more familiarly known as just the North Warwick Line, runs between Tyseley and Bearley North Junction where it connects with the GWR line from Hatton to Stratford-upon-Avon and Bristol (Temple Meads). The section between Stratford and Bristol closed in the 1960s. It was one of the last express routes to open in England, although the line's original promoters had no such grand ideas when proposals for the route were originally presented to Parliament.

The B&NW was originally conceived as a link between Stratford-upon-Avon and Birmingham, to connect with the GWR line to Honeybourne and Bristol and the Alcester branch at Aston Cantlow. A private company of local landowners and other members, was formed and a Bill deposited for the construction of a line from a new terminus in Birmingham, at Moor Street, to Stratford, a distance of 24 miles. The GWR raised objections because it feared competition for a shorter route to London than its own. This was a very real fear, as it turned out, because the Manchester, Sheffield and Lincolnshire Railway (later the Great Central Railway) was keen to operate the B&NW as a way of closing the gap between its then planned London extension, by obtaining running powers over the 22 miles of the bankrupt East and West Junction Railway. In the event, the scheme collapsed in 1898 when, as the GCR, it agreed terms with the GWR to improve its London approach to Marylebone, which also gave the Paddington company a shorter route from Birmingham to the capital.

The collapse of the GCR proposal left the B&NW company short of money and the line, although approved on 24 August 1894, was destined never to be constructed by its original promoters. It also never reached its projected length. By an Act of 9 August 1899, plans for an independent line between Birmingham and Stratford-upon-Avon were abandoned, the company settling for a line leaving the GWR just south of Tyseley, making it dependent on the Paddington company for access to Birmingham. Further problems arose when there was no capital for the project, the line only being saved when the GWR took over the scheme on 30 July 1900. The GWR gained further time to complete construction of the route and, a year later, authority was given for a second revision of the line. It was now to run from Tyseley and connect with the company's own line from Hatton, at Bearley North Junction. In this form, the B&NW opened to goods trains on 9 December 1907 and to passengers, using trains from Birmingham (Snow Hill), on 1 July 1908. From 1909, local trains over the route started from a new terminus at Birmingham (Moor Street), built under provisions in the original B&NW Act.

The new line was double-track from the outset, being useful as a shorter line to the West Country than the old route via Solihull and Hatton, and was 18 miles long. It had no major works except for one 175-yard tunnel at Wood End. The line runs through some of the most attractive Warwickshire countryside and immediately proved popular with passengers, some of whom moved out of smoky Birmingham and into the country, commuting to the city every day. Others visited such places as Earlswood Lakes, Henley-in-Arden and, of course, Stratford-upon-Avon itself. Thus, the line was well patronized from the beginning and justified GWR investment. After many scares since Dr Beeching scheduled the line for closure, the B&NW remains open and trains are still well filled with commuters and summer day-trippers.

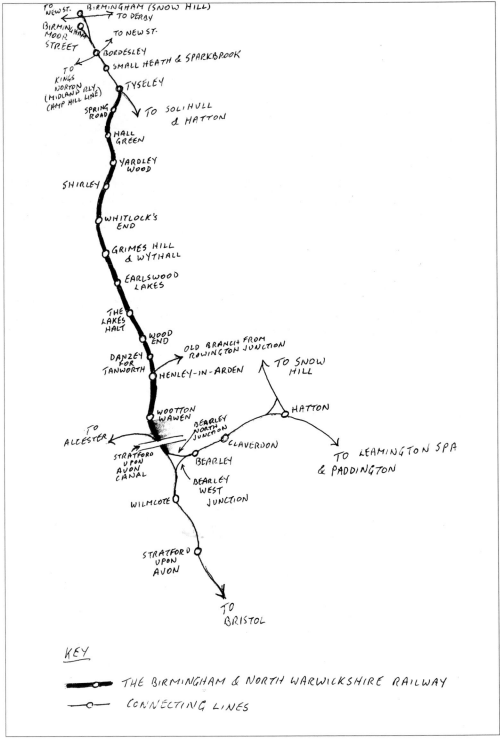

A map of the B&NW showing its connection from Tyseley and where it joins the B&OJ line, at Bearley North Junction, for Stratford-upon-Avon. Also in view is the line to Hatton and the route to Alcester.

An unidentified ex-GWR 'Hall' class 4–6–0 leaves the B&NW with a three-coach local from Stratford-upon-Avon in the early 1960s. In this view, the B&NW line curves sharply to the right, while the B&OJ main line to Paddington curves gently away on the left. To the right of the train are the Tyseley carriage sidings and goods lines.

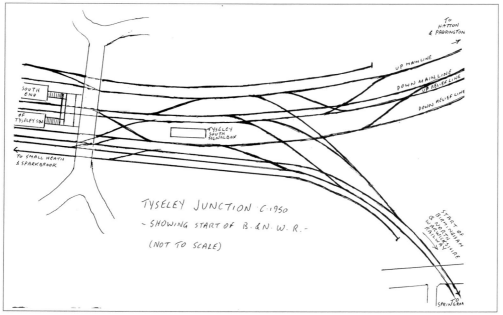

A plan of Tyseley Junction showing the start of the B&NW line curving sharply away at the bottom right.

After leaving Tyseley, the B&NW climbs virtually all the way to Earlswood Lakes, the peak of the line at 281 ft above sea level. The first station on the line is Spring Road Platform, seen here in the 1940s. The station lies in the Birmingham district of Tyseley and its two platforms served the Forman's Road factory of Joseph Lucas Ltd where car batteries were made, the company being an important manufacturer of car components.

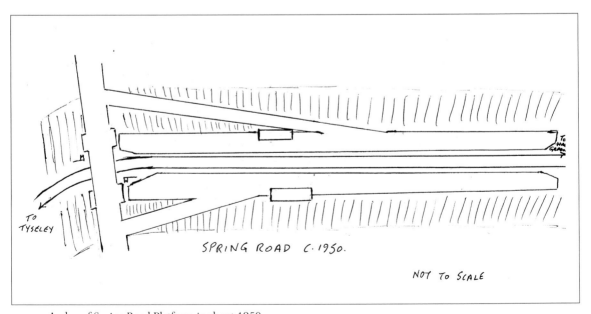

A plan of Spring Road Platform in about 1950.

Another 1940s view of Spring Road Platform. The station opened with the B&NW in 1908.

Spring Road on 8 January 1983. The 'Platform' had been dropped in the 1960s at a time when Lucas's built a car park over the railway, just before the line reached the station.

Just under a mile from Spring Road, the first important station is reached, at Hall Green. Hall Green station was provided with a brick-built main station building – 106 ft long, complete with GWR wooden canopy – on the Tyseley-bound platform and waiting room on the Stratford-bound platform. The long platforms were connected by a covered footbridge near the centre of the station. This footbridge continued to a footpath on the Stratford side which led to the main Stratford Road, which crosses the railway on a skew bridge. The station offices could only be approached from the platform. Sidings were provided at Hall Green on both Up and Down sides, with a goods shed behind the main Up platform. The Down sidings were near the signal-box which, in the summer of 1938, was open from 5.30 a.m. on Mondays until 1 a.m. the following Sunday morning, re-opening at 7 a.m. and closing at 11 p.m., with a long break from 1 p.m. to 7.30 p.m. The box was provided with a switch. Access to the goods sidings were at the Tyseley end of the station and crossing facilities from the Down to the Up line were under the skew bridge.

Another view of Hall Green station, looking towards Stratford-upon-Avon, showing the covered footbridge and skew bridge carrying the Stratford Road. Goods facilities at the station ceased on 6 May 1968 and all track was lifted. The whole area behind the main building is now a car park for a Park and Ride scheme for passengers travelling into Birmingham City centre. The buildings on the Down platform have been replaced by a 'bus shelter'-type structure, similar to most buildings on the B&NW.

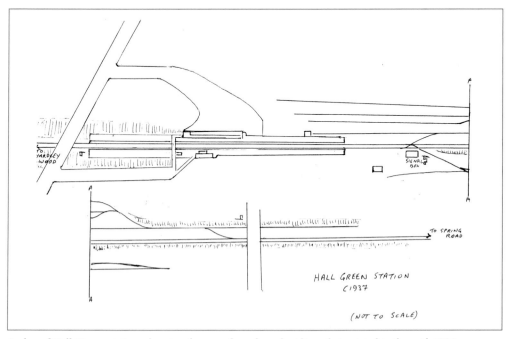

A plan of Hall Green station, showing the complex of goods sidings that existed in the mid-1930s.

A mile beyond Hall Green, the B&NW passes under a road bridge and enters the long-platformed Yardley Wood station, seen here looking towards Stratford. The station's booking office is situated on the road above, with ramps down to the platforms, where waiting accommodation is provided.

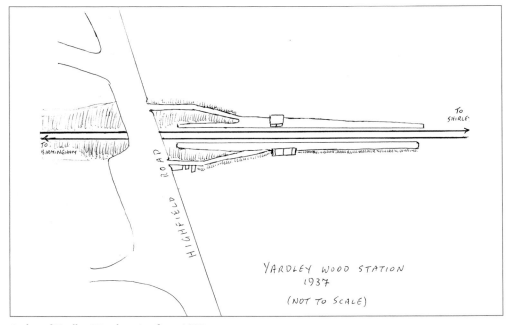

A plan of Yardley Wood station from 1937.

Yardley Wood station from the road overbridge shortly after the B&NW was opened. A rail motor train, made up of two coaches with a GWR 0–4–2 sandwiched in the middle, is passing with a local train to Birmingham, typifying the commuter trains of the day. The station is in a rural location which has long since disappeared. During the Blitz, the station was hit by a bomb, the blast demolishing six nearby shops.

Horse Show at Henley-in-Arden

MONDAY, AUGUST 1st

BOOKINGS TO
Earlswood Lakes, The Lakes Halt, Wood End, Danzey and Henley-in-Arden

FROM	Depart							RETURN FARES—THIRD CLASS				
								To Earlswood Lakes	To The Lakes Halt	To Wood End	To Danzey for Tanworth	To Henley in-Arden
	a.m.	a.m.	a.m.	a.m.	p.m.	p.m.	p.m.	s. d.	s. d.	s. d.	s. d.	s. d.
BIRMINGHAM (MOOR ST.)	9 20	9 35	10 15	11 30	12 25	1 20	2 30	1 4	1 6	1 7	1 7	2 1
Bordesley	9 24	9 38	10 20	11 33	12 28	1 23	2 33	1 4	1 4	1 6	1 7	2 1
Small Heath and Sparkbrook ..	9 28	9 41	10 25	11 36	12 31	1 26	2 36	1 1	1 3	1 4	1 7	1 7
Tyseley	9 32	9 45	10 30	11 39	12 35	1 30	2 39	1 0	1 1	1 3	1 6	1 7
Spring Road	9 36	9 48	10 35	11 42	12 38	1 33	2 42	11	1 0	1 1	1 4	1 7
Hall Green	9 40	9 51	10 39	11 45	12 41	1 36	2 45	9½	11	1 1	1 4	1 7
Yardley Wood	9 44	9 55	10 43	11 49	12 45	1 40	2 49	7½	9½	11	1 1	1 6

RETURN ARRANGEMENTS—SAME DAY

From Henley-in-Arden at 7.37, 8.10, 8.35 or 9.0 p.m.   From The Lakes Halt at 7.50, 8.50 or 9.15 p.m.
From Danzey at 7.43, 8.40 or 9.5 p.m.   From Earlswood Lakes at 7.55, 8.20, 8.53 or 9.18 p.m.
From Wood End at 7.48, 8.45 or 9.10 p.m.

A timetable for excursion trains to Henley-in-Arden from Birmingham (Moor Street) on August Bank Holiday, 1938.

On leaving Yardley Wood, the urbanized part of the B&NW is left behind and the line passes over
Baldwin's Lane on a brick-built overbridge. The scenery now becomes residential and semi-rural as the
line crosses the Birmingham City boundary and heads towards the second important station at Shirley, a
little over a mile beyond Yardley Wood. Serving a well-heeled town, Shirley station was substantial, with
brick buildings on both long platforms, covered by GWR wooden canopies. Iron picket fences backed the
platforms, as can be seen in this 1950s view. Behind the fence was a goods yard.

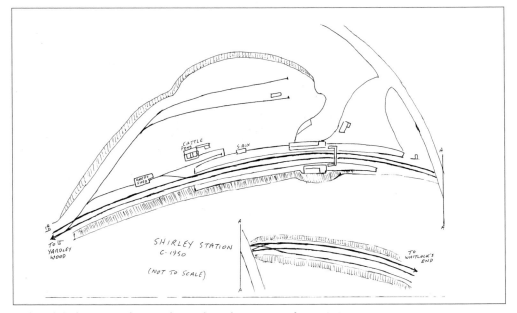

A plan of Shirley station showing the goods yard as it was in about 1950.

The Up side building at Shirley station as it appeared in April 1963. The entrance to the station is on the Down platform and both platforms are linked by a footbridge, which was a standard GWR type, covered in this view. This covering has since been removed.

The rear of the footbridge at Shirley station in April 1963. A crossover between the Up and Down running lines was provided at the Stratford end of the station. Many of the trains operating over the B&NW today terminate here.

The signal-box, situated on the Down platform at Shirley station, as it appeared in 1963. This box controlled the goods yard which was accessed from the Tyseley end of the station. Just visible beyond the signal-box is the goods shed.

A view of Shirley station goods yard in April 1963. On 6 May 1968, only five years later, this yard was closed.

On leaving Shirley station, the line passes under a road bridge and the scenery becomes rural. Three-quarters of a mile on and the B&NW enters Whitlock's End Halt, described by the GWR thus: 'This Halt consists of Up and Down platforms 300 feet each in length, standard height, and is situated 78 chains from Shirley station and 74 chains from Grimes Hill and Wythall station. Footpath approaches are provided from Tilehouse Lane and Houndsfield Lane to each platform.'

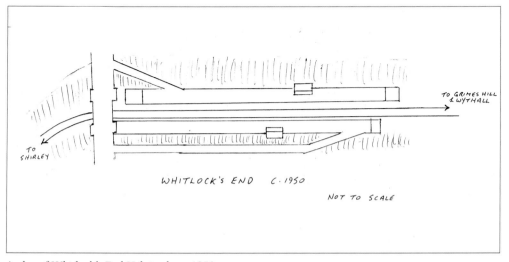

A plan of Whitlock's End Halt in about 1950.

Whitlock's End Halt, looking towards Stratford-upon-Avon, showing the simple wooden waiting shelters and access path. The Halt, along with The Lakes Halt, was opened by the GWR in 1936 in a bid to attract extra passengers to the line during the 'slump' period. At this point, the line is only 6 miles from Birmingham city centre.

The platform and waiting shelter at Whitlock's End, seen from a Stratford-bound train in June 1962.

Whitlock's End Halt as seen from the overbridge crossing the line, with a Birmingham-bound DMU waiting at the platform.

STRATFORD-ON-AVON and BIRMINGHAM.

Down. — Week Days

(timetable of train times between Stratford-on-Avon and Birmingham (Moor St.), with intermediate stations: Wilmcote, Bearley, Wootton Wawen Platform, Henley-in-Arden, Danzey for Tanworth, Wood End, Earlswood Lakes, Grimes Hill and Wythall, Shirley, Yardley Wood, Hall Green, Spring Road, Tyseley 103, Small Heath A, Bordesley, Birmingham (Moor St.), 108, 139 (Snow H.))

Down. — Wk Days—cont'd. / Sundays.

Legend / notes:

A Small Heath & Sparkbrook
Aa Stops at 7 58 p.m. to set down only
E or Ɛ Except Saturdays
S or Ş Saturdays only
X or χ Third class only.
Limited accommodation
B Third class only
¶ "Halts" at The Lakes between Wood End and Earlswood Lakes, and at Whitlock's End between Grimes...

A timetable for trains operating along the B&NW in November 1947.

From Whitlock's End, the B&NW passes through rolling north Warwickshire countryside as it approaches Grimes Hill and Wythall Platform, simply called 'Wythall' since 6 May 1974. Before reaching the station, a sand quarry is visible on the right, sand-martins being frequently seen flitting in and out of the sand walls. Approached on a sweeping curve, Grimes Hill and Wythall has a short platform on each side of the line and all buildings are single-storey wooden and corrugated-iron structures in use as waiting rooms. The corrugated-iron waiting room on the Down platform can be seen in this view. Access to the station is down ramps from the road above which crosses the railway at the Stratford end, as seen here. A wooden ticket office was situated at the top of the ramp to the Up platform. Since the mid-1970s, the old station buildings have been replaced by 'bus-shelter'-type structures. The B&NW has always had to compete with the services along its route. In Birmingham, the city's own buses have served such places as Tyseley, Yardley Wood and Hall Green, while the Birmingham and Midland Motor Omnibus Company, better known as the Midland Red, has long since operated an hourly service between Birmingham and Stratford-upon-Avon, via Shirley, Henley-in-Arden and Wootton Wawen. The Midland Red also operated an Evesham–Birmingham service through Wythall and a single-decker bus service from the parish church at Wythall to Shirley. Although it took a rather circuitous route which, incidentally, passed Grimes Hill and Wythall station, its advantage was that it connected with Birmingham buses bound for the city centre, at the Maypole, and went on to the heart of Shirley shopping centre, something the railway cannot do. Another Midland Red service operated between Birmingham and Earlswood.

Grimes Hill and Wythall platform showing the wooden ticket office at the top of the ramp above the Up platform. When the wooden buildings were still standing on the Up platform, an iron stove was used for heating during the winter months and passengers on cold mornings would be greeted by a cosy waiting room, and a stove glowing a dull red. This was particularly welcome after a long walk to the station to catch a train for work in Birmingham. The ticket collector, who was the only member of staff by the early 1970s, must have arrived very early in the morning to light that stove and passengers were certainly grateful to him.

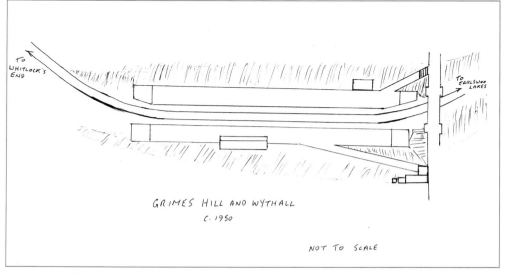

A 1950s plan of Grimes Hill and Wythall station.

After leaving Grimes Hill and Wythall, the B&NW makes the final ascent, at 1 in 150, to Earlswood Lakes station. Situated at the top of the long banks from both Birmingham and Stratford-upon-Avon, watering facilities were provided for locomotives here in steam days, the water tank being placed behind the Up platform, seen in this view. The station was substantially built, with brick structures on both long platforms. The main building was on the Down platform. A standard steel footbridge connected both platforms. The station was provided with a spacious goods yard which contained a single, long siding for coal traders, a short dock and a 'loop' siding. Attached to the Down platform, towards the Stratford end, opposite to this view, was a small goods shed. The signal-box was just beyond the Stratford end of the Up platform and, in the summer of 1938, was open continuously. Goods traffic at the station ceased on 6 July 1964, and the station buildings were removed in the mid-1970s, leaving an open space where these buildings had been. The station was renamed Earlswood from 6 May 1974. Loss of the express service that operated over the B&NW in the early 1960s, as part of the Beeching Plan and a general decline in local passenger traffic as car ownership increased during the same period, brought the future of the line into question when BR announced closure from 5 May 1969. However, the North Warwickshire Line Action Group was established to save the line. Several years of action did eventually save the line when the High Court demanded that it remain open. There have been a few threats since but the B&NW is still not really secure, although there are plans to utilize it as part of a new 'Cross-City' route, via Birmingham (Snow Hill) to Stourbridge Junction.

The Up platform looking towards Stratford-upon-Avon, showing the Earlswood signal-box just beyond. The station is situated in a leisure area of three lakes, which has long been popular with tourists from Birmingham, thanks to vigorous advertising by the GWR who pointed out the attractions of the line. Unfortunately those using Earlswood Lakes station had a long, although leafy, walk through Earls Wood to reach the lakes, while those 'in the know' continued their journey to The Lakes Halt, which was right next to them.

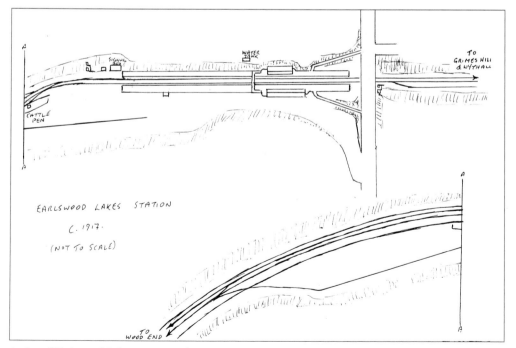

A plan of Earlswood Lakes station in about 1917.

After leaving Earlswood Lakes the B&NW begins to descend, at a gradient of 1 in 150/180, towards Stratford-upon-Avon, with only a short climb beyond Wootton Wawen to Wilmcote to negotiate. The line called next at The Lakes Halt, which opened in 1936 and is shown here, looking similar to Whitlock's End. The GWR described it thus: 'This Halt consists of Up and Down platforms 130 feet each in length, standard height, and is situated 70 chains from Earlswood Lakes station and 1 mile 5¾ chains from Wood End station.'

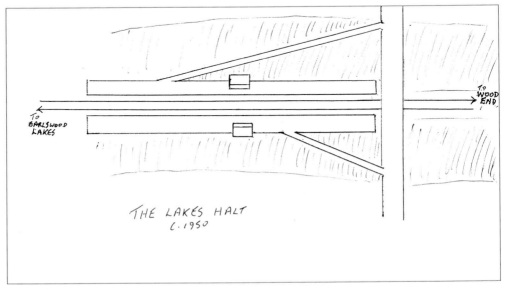

A plan of The Lakes Halt in about 1950.

Wood End station looking towards Stratford-upon-Avon in about 1950. After passing through Wood End station, the B&NW travels through the only major structure over the whole route, the 175-yard Wood End Tunnel, before reaching Danzey station.

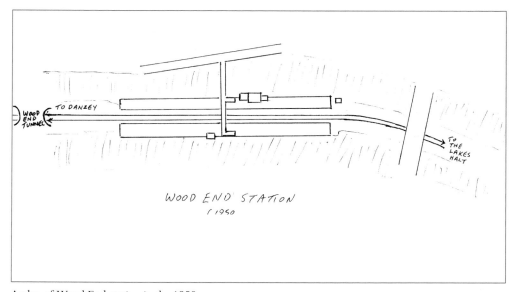

A plan of Wood End station in the 1950s.

Just under 2 miles beyond Wood End Tunnel, Danzey station is reached. This was an original B&NW station which was given the name, 'Danzey for Tanworth'. The station took its name from nearby Danzey Green but also served the nearby village of Tanworth-in-Arden. Since 6 May 1974, the station has been known just as 'Danzey'. From the opening of the B&NW, the GWR operated West Country expresses over the route from Wolverhampton (Low Level) and Birmingham (Snow Hill) and the line saw Churchward 'County' class 4–4–0s on such trains until replaced by 'Star' class 4–6–0s after the Second World War, and 'Castle' class 4–6–0s in the 1950s. The line was also well used by heavy coal trains from the South Wales mines along with other freight trains. In the 1930s AEC diesel railcars, built for the GWR, were seen on local services and Cardiff expresses. Local trains became operated by DMUs from 1957 when Derby-built class 116s were introduced to the B&NW and steam gradually vanished from the line.

The goods yard at Danzey for Tanworth station, complete with corrugated, barn-like, goods shed. The goods yard closed on 1 July 1964, this picture being taken shortly afterwards.

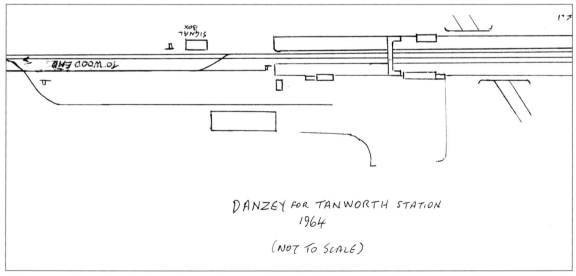

A plan of Danzey for Tanworth station and goods yard in 1964.

Danzey for Tanworth station, looking towards Wood End, showing the signal-box and GWR lower quadrant signal at clear.

The corrugated-iron waiting room on the Down platform at Danzey for Tanworth as it appeared in July 1964.

The main station building on the Up platform at Danzey for Tanworth in July 1964. Like the waiting room on the Down platform, this structure was also built of corrugated iron. Also in view is the staircase of the concrete footbridge connecting the platform.

A view of the entrance to Danzey for Tanworth station from the concrete footbridge in July 1964. Also in view is the Up platform station building.

Danzey signal-box, a typical GWR structure, as it appeared in July 1964.

The acute-angled bridge which carries the B&NW over a minor road just south of Danzey for Tanworth station, as it appeared in 1958.

From Danzey for Tanworth, the B&NW runs a further 3 miles down towards the largest, and most impressive, station on the whole of the route at Henley-in-Arden, seen here in the 1950s looking towards Stratford-upon-Avon. Henley-in-Arden B&NW station replaced the one from Rowington Junction which closed on 1 July 1908 as the new one opened, and was provided with a platform on the Down side on which were substantial brick buildings containing the main station entrance, the ticket office, waiting rooms and all other facilities. The Up line was served by an island platform with its own buildings, both platforms being linked by a covered footbridge. In its heyday, the station had flowerbeds which were tended by the station staff. They were so well looked after that the station often won awards, given by the GWR, for the Best Kept Station. The B&NW station was for passengers only, goods traffic using the old station via a stub from the B&NW. Goods services ceased at Henley-in-Arden on 31 December 1962; the station itself, of course, still remains open.

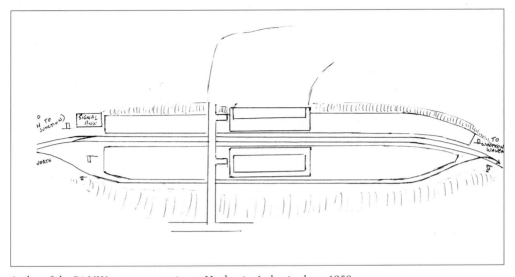

A plan of the B&NW passenger station at Henley-in-Arden in about 1950.

After leaving Henley-in-Arden the B&NW continues down the bank and into Wootten Wawen Platform. Wootton Wawen is known locally for its large, residential, mobile-home park, some of those living there using the little station. In recent times, Wootten Wawen has been threatened with closure, BR planning to terminate B&NW trains at Henley-in-Arden, passengers for Stratford going via Solihull, Hatton and Bearley. This would leave Wootten Wawen isolated from the rail network. The station at Wootton Wawen is seen here in the 1950s.

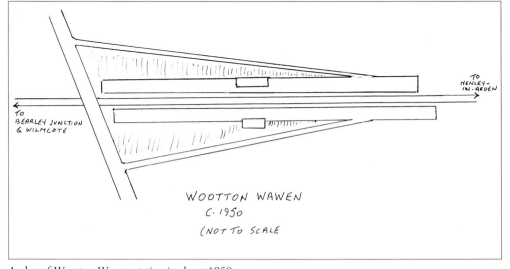

A plan of Wootton Wawen station in about 1950.

Wootton Wawen Platform, showing waiting shelters built of the favourite GWR material for small halts, corrugated iron. From Wootton Wawen, the line heads towards Bearley North Junction, where it joins the B&OJ to Stratford-upon-Avon. Just before reaching the junction, the trackbed of the old line to Alcester is visible on the right. The B&NW then passes under the iron Edstone Viaduct which carries the Stratford-upon-Avon Canal just a few yards short of Bearley North Junction, where the B&NW ends.

MONDAY, AUGUST 1st

BOOKINGS TO

Stratford-on-Avon
Evesham, Fladbury and Pershore

(Via North Warwickshire Line)

FROM	To Stratford-on-Avon and Evesham only	To Stratford, Evesham Fladbury and Pershore	To Stratford-on-Avon only	To Evesham Fladbury and Pershore	To Stratford-on-Avon only	To Stratford-on-Avon only	To Stratford, Evesham Fladbury and Pershore	To Stratford-on-Avon only	To Stratford-on-Avon only	RETURN FARES THIRD CLASS To Stratford-on-Avon	To Evesham, Fladbury Pershore
	a.m.	a.m.	a.m.	a.m.	a.m.	a.m.	p.m.	p.m.	p.m.	s. d.	s. d.
Wolverhampton (L.L.)	—	8 57	—	9 15	9 35	10A23	—	—	—	4 2	See p. 16
Bilston (G.W.)	—	9 4	—	9 22	9 42	10A17	—	—	—	3 8	for Book'gs
Wednesbury	—	9 10	—	9 28	9 49	10A23	—	—	—	3 8	4 9
Swan Village	—	9 14	—	—	—	10A27	—	—	—	3 8	4 2
West Bromwich	—	9 18	—	9 36	9 57	10A31	—	—	—	3 2	4 2
Handsworth (G.W.)	—	9 23	—	9 41	10 3	10A36	—	—	—	3 2	4 2
Soho & Winson Grn.	—	9 27	—	9 45	—	—	—	—	—	3 2	3 8
Hockley	9 10	9 31	9 45	9 49	10 8	—	—	—	—	2 8	3 8
BIRMINGH'M (S.H.)	9 20	9 40	9 55	9 58	10 17	11 15	12 5	12M25	1 35	2 8	3 8
Bordesley	9 25	9 45	9 59	10 3	10 22	—	12 9	12 28	1 39	2 8	3 8
Small Hth. & Spk'bk	9 30	9 50	10 3	10 8	10 25	—	12 13	12 31	1 44	2 8	3 8
Tyseley	9 34	9 55	10 7	10 13	10 30	—	12 17	12 35	1 48	2 8	3 8
Spring Road	—	—	—	10 17	10 35	—	—	12 38	—	2 8	3 8
Hall Green	—	—	—	10 21	10 39	—	—	12 41	—	—	3 8
Yardley Wood	—	—	—	10 26	10 43	—	—	12 45	—	2 6	3 8
Stratford-on-Avon	10 15	10 31	—	—	—	—	12 57	—	2 32	—	1 7

A—Change at Birmingham (Snow Hill).   M—This Train departs from Birmingham (MOOR STREET STATION).

RETURN ARRANGEMENTS SAME DAY	From Pershore	From Fladbury	From Evesham	From Stratford-on-Avon
To Stratford-on-Avon	6.45, 7.45 or 9.5 p.m.	6.52, 7.53 or 9.13 p.m.	7.5, 8.5 or 9.25 p.m.	—
To Yardley Wood, Hall Green and Spring Road	9.5 p.m.	9.13 p.m.	9.25 p.m.	8.20, or 9.50 p.m.
To Tyseley, Small Heath, Bordesley and Birmingham (Snow Hill)	6.45, 7.45 or 9.5 p.m.	6.52, 7.53 or 9.13 p.m.	7.5, 8.5 or 9.25 p.m.	7.5, 7.35, 8.32, 8B50 or 9.50 p.m.
To Hockley, Soho, Handsworth, West Bromwich, Swan Village, Wednesbury, Bilston and Wolverhampton (Low Level)	7.45 or 9.5 p.m.	7.53 or 9.13 p.m.	8.5 or 9.25 p.m.	8.32, 8.50 or 9.50 p.m.

An August Bank Holiday timetable for excursions via the B&NW in 1938.

In 1966, BR closed the locoshed at Tyseley and it was demolished, leaving only a turntable and coaling stage. This coaling stage was taken over by the Standard Gauge Steam Trust to house the recently acquired ex-GWR 'Castle' class 4–6–0 no. 7029 *Clun Castle*. Following funding by Birmingham City Council, the area became known as the Birmingham Railway Museum, and the number of locos, rolling stock and other railway artefacts increased. Restoration work was carried out at Tyseley, including full restoration of another 'Castle', no. 5080 *Defiant* and ex-LMS 'Jubilee' class 4–6–0 no. 5583 *Kolhapur*. Tyseley became important as a servicing and turning point for steam excursions from Didcot to Birmingham along the B&OJ, as well as trains from Marylebone to Stratford-upon-Avon. In its time, the museum has handled some of the most famous, preserved steam locos running on the main line, including ex-LNER Pacific *Flying Scotsman*, ex-LMS 'Princess-Royal' Pacifics and Duchess Pacific *Duchess of Hamilton*. Tyseley has also organized steam excursions, using its own steam locos *Clun Castle* and *Kolhapur* along the B&NW line to Stratford-upon-Avon. In June 1985, these two locos were involved in such trips to celebrate the 150th anniversary of the Great Western Railway. Here, in 1985, several of the museum's collection of locos and rolling stock are grouped around the turntable at Tyseley.

Also in 1985 a pair of Tyseley museum's ex-GWR 0–6–0 pannier tanks are posed round the turntable. Just visible behind is replica GWR Broad Gauge loco *North Star*, specially built for the GWR anniversary celebrations.

At the head of a train at the Tyseley museum is ex-LNER Thompson B1 4–6–0 no. 1306 *Mayflower*. This loco ran up and down a short length of track, giving passenger rides, in June 1985.

Ex-Taff Vale Railway 0–6–2 tank loco no. 28 runs through Birmingham Railway Museum, Tyseley in June 1985, with a demonstration goods train.

One year later and another tank loco, ex-Metropolitan Railway 0–4–4T no. 1 rests on the little passenger line at the Tyseley museum while operating the shuttle.

Over the weekend of 8 and 9 June 1985, Birmingham Railway Museum operated trains between Tyseley and Stratford-upon-Avon, via the B&NW, as part of the GWR anniversary celebrations, using *Clun Castle* and *Kolhapur*. Unfortunately, *Kolhapur* developed a 'hot box' in her tender axle and had to be withdrawn after her first trip, leaving *Clun Castle* to operate all of the services. On Saturday 8 June, trains started from Hall Green station and *Clun Castle* is seen at the station, passing a DMU which has just arrived from Stratford.

A photostop was made at Henley-in-Arden and *Clun Castle* is seen waiting to depart with The Shakespeare Express from Tyseley on 8 June 1985.

Another view of *Clun Castle* at Henley-in-Arden on 8 June 1985. The loco had recently been overhauled and outshopped in her true BR livery, instead of the GWR colours in which she had been originally preserved. This was not the first time that the Birmingham Railway Museum had run an excursion along the B&NW. Shortly after becoming a steam approved route, the museum ran an excursion along the line on Sunday 13 May 1973 using ex-GWR 0–6–0 pannier tank no. 7752.

After the success of the 1985 B&NW excursions, with the trains carrying over 3,000 passengers, Birmingham Railway Museum operated further trains, also called The Shakespeare Express, on the weekend of 7/8 June 1986. Here *Clun Castle* is seen entering Tyseley station with the first train from Stratford-upon-Avon on 7 June 1986.

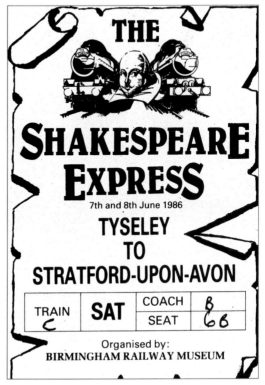

A ticket for The Shakespeare Express excursions in 1985.

Approaching Stratford-upon-Avon behind *Clun Castle* on 7 June 1986. Ex-LMS 'Jubilee' 4–6–0 no. 5593 *Kolhapur* is seen waiting to return to Tyseley with the second train of the day.

Kolhapur is ready to depart from Stratford-upon-Avon with The Shakespeare Express from Stratford-upon-Avon on 7 June 1986. This ex-LMS loco had undergone a £70,000 restoration in 1985 especially for the B&NW trips, but the axle-box problem caused her withdrawal that year. However, the following year she ran all of her trips without any problems. In 1987, further trips were run, using newly restored 'Castle' class 4–6–0 no. 5080 *Defiant* and *Clun Castle*. These trips were run in October of that year.

OTHER RAILWAYS IN WARWICKSHIRE

Two other companies also had routes which ran through Warwickshire. These were the Great Central Railway, whose line from London (Marylebone) to Manchester and Sheffield ran through the county at Rugby, and the Midland Railway, who had a route from Birmingham to Leicester, via Nuneaton. The company also had a line through Stratford-upon-Avon, as the Stratford-upon-Avon and Midland Junction Railway. This latter line met the GCR at Woodford and ran to Broom Junction (for Evesham). The section from Woodford to Stratford-upon-Avon was once part of the East and West Junction Railway, and the route by which the GCR would have had access to Marylebone to Birmingham, via the planned Birmingham and North Warwickshire Railway.

The GCR came to Warwickshire in 1899, its station at Rugby being situated well away from the town centre. The railway did give Rugby outlets to Yorkshire, Newcastle-on-Tyne, Hull, South Wales and Southampton; it also tapped rail traffic from Rugby almost as soon as it opened. The GCR closed in the 1960s, as part of Dr Beeching's rationalization plans.

The Midland Railway route between Birmingham and Leicester opened in 1864, with stations at Whitacre, Shustoke, Arley, Stockingford and Nuneaton. The first station at Nuneaton had a short life of only nine years. It was replaced by another building, 150 yards further west, to make way for the joint MR/LNWR Ashby–Nuneaton line, opened in 1873. This station became Nuneaton Abbey at the 'Grouping'. Like the GCR, Abbey station no longer exists, although the line is still open and still carries passengers.

The LNWR had a virtual monopoly of services at Rugby until the Manchester, Sheffield and Lincolnshire Railway decided to build its own line to London (Marylebone), which was to run via Rugby. This line was opened in 1907, at a time when the MS&L changed its name to the Great Central Railway. The prospect of competition to the LNWR at Rugby was favourably greeted by businessmen in the town, but they were to be disappointed when the station was created half a mile further out of Rugby than that of the LNWR. The GCR, however, did give Rugby a useful outlet to the West Riding of Yorkshire, Newcastle, Hull, South Wales, the south-west of England and the south of England, particularly Southampton. The GCR began tapping Rugby traffic from its opening. In this view, a GCR Robinson 4–4–0 waits at Rugby with a London train.

The ex-GCR station at Rugby in BR days. BR named the station 'Rugby Central', which was rather ironic as it was actually placed right on the boundary of the town.

Another view of the ex-GCR station at Rugby in the 1950s.

A view, shortly after opening, of the GCR station at Woodford Halse, on the Woodford and Hinton Junction. All of the GCR stations on its London line were, unusually, island platforms.

The entrance to the GCR station at Woodford Halse in BR days. As the station had only island platforms, access had to be via a subway from the road below. The GCR main line was closed in the mid-1960s.

Stratford-upon-Avon (old station) on the Stratford and Midland Junction Railway, previously the East and West Junction Railway. The railway was conceived as a freight route linking Northamptonshire with Bristol, chiefly for the carriage of iron ore. The line did, however, have a passenger service, which lasted until 1952. Freight services continued until the line was closed in 1965. The station was a curious place with an abandoned signal-box, a legacy of the East and West Junction Railway, situated behind the operational box. The station also had an unusual platform canopy. The locoshed here is just visible on the right, behind the carriages and platform building. The E&WJR was always in financial trouble and was eager to link up with the M&SL who were keen to gain access to Birmingham via the proposed B&NW. They were eventually thwarted by the GWR.

A view of the derelict station of the S&MJ at Stratford-upon-Avon (old town) after the line had closed to passengers. This shows the main building, minus a canopy, and the vandalized signal-box.

Another view of the S&MJ station at Stratford-upon-Avon, after closure to passengers.

The S&MJ locoshed at Stratford-upon-Avon as it appeared in June 1965. The shed had officially closed in February 1953, but in January 1954 six or seven ex-LMS class 4F 0–6–0s were often kept there overnight for use on freight trains that still operated out of the town.

A side view of the S&MJ shed at Stratford-upon-Avon in June 1965.

Two locos, ex-LMS 4F 0–6–0 no. 44103 and ex-LNWR 7F 0–8–0 no. 49342, wait with freight trains at Abbey Junction, Nuneaton on 11 September 1954. This junction was built by the Midland Railway in 1880, to link its line from Birmingham to Leicester with the LNWR Trent Valley Railway.

Ex-LMS locos come off the Ashby Junction line at Nuneaton, having run from Weddington Junction on the Ashby and Nuneaton joint LNWR/MR line on 11 September 1954. The engines in question are ex-LMS 8F 2–8–0 no. 48657 and Hughes-Fowler 'Crab' 2–6–0 no. 42885.

Ex-Midland Railway 3F 0–6–0 no. 43728 waits at the ex-MR station at Nuneaton Abbey after bringing in an excursion train on 14 April 1957. The MR line between Birmingham and Leicester, on which the Nuneaton Abbey station was situated, opened in 1864.

Nuneaton Abbey Street station as it appeared in the 1950s. The first Midland Railway station at Nuneaton had a short life of only nine years, being replaced by one built 150 yards further west to make way for the Ashby and Nuneaton line. This was a joint LNWR/MR venture which opened in 1873 and became Nuneaton Abbey Street station at the 1923 'Grouping'.

A 1950s view of Nuneaton Abbey Street station. This station closed on 4 March 1968, along with the ex-MR line to Birmingham. In 1971, the Ashby–Nuneaton joint line was also closed. The only station that remains open at Nuneaton is the one on the Trent Valley Railway, which remains busy with TVR traffic and trains to Coventry.

ACKNOWLEDGEMENTS

I should like to record my grateful thanks to all who helped in putting this book together, especially Roger Carpenter who supplied many of the photographs. Thanks also to David Ibbotson and the Reverend David Hardy for the material they supplied. I also thank Alwen and Gary for their continued support of all my efforts.